The Future of Israel

A Biblical Prophetic Perspective

Pastor Jan Voerman

TEACH Services, Inc.
PUBLISHING
www.TEACHServices.com • (800) 367-1844

World rights reserved. This book or any portion thereof may not be copied or reproduced in any form or manner whatever, except as provided by law, without the written permission of the publisher, except by a reviewer who may quote brief passages in a review.

The author assumes full responsibility for the accuracy of all facts and quotations as cited in this book. The opinions expressed in this book are the author's personal views and interpretations, and do not necessarily reflect those of the publisher.

This book is provided with the understanding that the publisher is not engaged in giving spiritual, legal, medical, or other professional advice. If authoritative advice is needed, the reader should seek the counsel of a competent professional.

Copyright © 2016 Jan Voerman

Copyright © 2016 TEACH Services, Inc.

ISBN-13: 978-1-4796-0679-5 (Paperback)
ISBN-13: 978-1-4796-0680-1 (ePub)
ISBN-13: 978-1-4796-0681-8 (Mobi)

Library of Congress Control Number: 2016904402

Unless otherwise indicated, all Scripture quotations are from the King James Version (KJV).

Scripture quotations marked AMP are from the *Amplified Bible*, Copyright © 1954, 1958, 1962, 1964, 1965, 1987 by The Lockman Foundation. Used by permission.

Scripture quotations marked "Berkeley Version" are from the *Holy Bible. The Berkeley Version in Modern English, Containing the Old and New Testaments; Translated afresh from the Original Languages and Diligently Compared with Previous Translations; With Numerous Helpful Non-Doctrinal Notes to Aid the Understanding of the Reader*. Grand Rapids: Zondervan, 1959, translated by Gerrit Verkuyl, 1951.

Scripture quotations marked CEB are from the *Common English Bible New Testament*, Copyright © 2010 by Common English Bible.

Scripture quotations marked ESV are from *The Holy Bible, English Standard Version*, Copyright © 2001 by Crossway Bibles, a publishing ministry of Good News Publishers.

Scripture quotations marked JB are from *The Jerusalem Bible*, Copyright © 1966 by Darton Longman & Todd Ltd and Doubleday and Company Ltd.

Scripture quotations marked Moffatt are from *The Bible: James Moffatt Translation*, Copyright © 1922, 1924, 1925, 1926, 1935 Harper Collins San Francisco, Copyright © 1950, 1952, 1953, 1954 James A. R. Moffatt.

Scripture quotations marked NASB are from the *New American Standard Bible*, Copyright © 1960, 1962, 1963, 1968, 1971, 1972, 1973, 1975, 1977, 1995 by The Lockman Foundation.

Scripture quotations marked NEB are from *The New English Bible*, Copyright © 1961 Oxford University Press and Cambridge University Press.

Scripture quotations marked NIV are from *The Holy Bible, New International Version®*, NIV® Copyright © 1973, 1978, 1984 by Biblica, Inc.® Used by permission. All rights reserved worldwide.

Scripture quotations marked NKJV are from the *New King James Version®*. Copyright © 1982 by Thomas Nelson. Used by permission. All rights reserved.

Scripture quotations marked Weymouth are from the *Weymouth New Testament*, Richard Francis Weymouth, 1912. Public domain in the United States.

Italicized words in the *King James Version* (KJV), the *Amplified Bible* (AMP) and the *New King James Version* (NKJV) are in the original text and indicate words added by the translators.

Published by

www.TEACHServices.com • (800) 367-1844

Jan Voerman is also author of

The Hidden Agenda (2006)

Secret Messages in the Church (2013)

Ellen White & the Trinity (2013)

The Ordination of Women (2014)

Raising a Red Flag (2014)

Contents

Introduction.. 7

Part 1 A POPULAR VIEW OF ISRAEL IN PROPHECY... 9
    Dispensationalism.................................10
    Israel's Restoration..............................12
    Did Christ Project an Earthly Kingdom?............13
    Cyrus I. Scofield, Promoter of Dispensationalism......15
    Scofield's Young Adult Life.......................17
    Hitting Bottom 18
    Divorce and Remarriage............................20
    Ordained a Minister...............................21
    Without Academic Training.........................22
    Origins of Futurism...............................23
    Dispensationalism's Counter-Reformation Roots......24
    Biblical Interpretation with an Agenda.............25
    Segregated Rewards?...............................26
    The Secret of the Rapture.........................28
    Not Taught by the Apostles........................29
    "Consider ... Their Way of Life"..................30
    Controversial Connections.........................31
    Summing Up..32

Part 2 ISRAEL AND THE NEW TESTAMENT.......... 33
    Jesus and John the Baptist Announce
    the Kingdom of God................................34
    The Fruitless Fig Tree............................36
    A Decisive Moment.................................38
    A Clear and Lasting Sentence......................39
    Two Sons, Two Responses...........................40
    The Last and Best.................................42
    Undeserving Wedding Guests........................43
    When "My House" Became "Your House"...............46
    Children of the Flesh Vs. Children of the Promise.....49
    A Nighttime Visit.................................50
    The End of Jewish Segregation.....................52
    A Different Blessing for Jews and Gentiles?.........55
    A People in Bondage...............................58
    Desiring a Heavenly Country.......................60

    A Divine Revelation Pronounces Gentiles Clean. 62
    A Surprising Element in Israel's Recovery 64
    Circumcised Inside 67
    The Olive Tree. 69
    "All" of Which "Israel"? 72
    Paul's Continual Sorrow 74
    The Meaning of the "Gentile Fullness" 76
    A Blessed Period of Restoration for the Jews? 78
    The "Second Chance" is Today 81
    Too Late Once the Door is Shut 83
    An Obsolete Ceremonial System Revived? 86
    Jesus' Two Ways ... Plus One? 88
    The Times of the Gentiles. 90

Part 3   **Israel and the Old Testament** **95**
    God's Covenant of Grace. 96
    The Promised Land. 98
    God Doesn't Play Favorites. .99
    The "If" of God's Oath 103
    Blessings or Curses 107
    Probationary Time 109
    Twofold Messages 114
    A Plan for All the Faithful 116
    Scattered and Dispersed. 119
    Another Return? 121
    "Last Days" Already in the Past. 123
    The Ten Tribes and the Rebuilding of Israel. 127
    Zechariah's Prophecy of the Future 130
    What Makes the New Covenant New 133
    Will Jerusalem Have a Glorious Recovery? 135
    God's Chosen People 140

Appendix **145**

Introduction

Down through the centuries, Israel has played a significant role in world history and Christian theology. During this time, they have experienced many ups and downs of great blessings and great distress and repeated setbacks. They were taken into captivity to learn the lesson of trusting the God of their fathers, and the Lord God has been very gracious to them in gathering them back again into the Promised Land.

Israel has been involved in many wars. Yet, God has fought for them, and they have conquered mighty nations. In several periods of their history, Israel has been prosperous, strong and mighty, a nation feared by the surrounding peoples. God chose Israel as His special elect, and He has done many wonderful things for His people, giving them great promises on condition of obedience. However, on the whole, the report of Israel's history has been rather sad, with judgments and punishment. Frequently they have been ruled by other nations. Yet, Israel has survived to this day, and there are promises remaining that were never completely fulfilled because of Israel's failure to comply with the conditions. So, will these prophecies still be fulfilled? Is there any hope that God will once again bless Israel and look after them as He did in days of old? Will He gather them together into the land that He swore to their fathers that He would give them as their possession? Will Israel be built and established again as a mighty, holy nation, and will they be converted and accept their Messiah, fulfilling their mission as a channel of blessing to other nations during the millennial kingdom, as many people believe will take place? Does the Bible provide us with evidence that all this will indeed come true? How should we understand the prophecies of the Old Testament about Israel's promised recovery in the Promised Land?

In this book, we will explore these questions, which occupy the thoughts of so many, and we will seek biblical answers. I pray that, through this book, you will gain a greater understanding of this important topic and be blessed for having read it.

Pastor Jan Voerman
The Netherlands

Part 1

A POPULAR VIEW OF ISRAEL IN PROPHECY

Dispensationalism

There is a great interest these days in the nation of Israel. The most prolific prophetic view of Israel, which has been popularized in recent decades by Christian writers Hal Lindsey and by the "Left Behind" series of Tim LaHaye and Jerry B. Jenkins, has as its base a system of biblical interpretation known as *dispensationalism*. This system divides biblical history into seven time periods, or "dispensations," each having its own unique characteristics and particular way that God related to humans.

According to this system, the **first** of these seven periods was the Edenic dispensation of **innocence**, the period before the Fall, which ended in judgment and Adam and Eve's expulsion from paradise. The **second** period was the dispensation of **conscience**, which ended in the judgment of the Flood. The **third** period was the dispensation of **human government**, which ended with the building of a city and the tower of Babel with God's judgment of dispersion over the face of the planet. The **fourth** dispensation was the period of **promise**. In it, God called Abraham with the promise that through him all nations would be blessed. The blessing would come through his only son Isaac, who was the child of promise. Isaac's younger son Jacob was chosen by God and received the name "Israel," which means "God prevails." Israel's twelve sons grew into the twelve tribes of Israel. The fourth period ended with God's judgment and Israel's bondage in Egypt.

The **fifth** period in the dispensational system was the dispensation of **law,** during which time God entered into covenant relationship with Israel at Sinai and gave them His law through Moses, Israel's first national leader. Under the next leader Joshua, they entered the Promised Land. Next came the period of the judges, after which the children of Israel asked for a king to rule over them. Saul was selected the first king of Israel. David succeeded him. David's son Solomon built a temple for God. After Solomon's reign, the kingdom of Israel was divided into a northern part, composed of ten tribes, and a southern part, composed of the tribes of Judah and Benjamin. Nineteen kings ruled over the ten tribes of the house of Israel until the Assyrian captivity in the year 722 BC. Twenty different kings reigned over the southern dual-tribe kingdom of Judah until the Babylonian captivity in the year 586 BC, when Jerusalem was destroyed. It would seem appropriate to begin a new dispensation at this point, for, as with previous periods, God acted in judgment—the judgment of captivity. However, this time, there is no new dispensation.

After seventy years of captivity, there was a period of rebuilding.

After seventy years of captivity, there was a period of rebuilding. God had compassion on His people, and they were called to return to the Promised Land. In spite of hostile opposition from their enemies, God blessed them, and the nations surrounding Israel perceived that God was with them in their rebuilding activities (Neh. 6:16). This new beginning was a very significant moment in Israel's history, and yet no new dispensation is recognized at this point. Why not?

This new beginning was a very significant moment in Israel's history, and yet no new dispensation is recognized at this point. Why not?

Why are there seven dispensations and not eight, nine or ten? Philip Mauro, who was a dispensationalist for many years, explained in chapter two of his book, *The Gospel of the Kingdom,* that the method by which these dispensations "have been arrived at is purely arbitrary, fanciful, and destitute of scriptural support ..."[1] The arbitrary nature of the divisions would indicate that one person's division of Bible history into dispensations is about as valid as another's. This is certainly something to think about. Before accepting this system of interpretation as biblically true, as so many people have easily seemed to do, it would be well worth testing its validity carefully.

The fifth dispensation continued until the crucifixion of Christ and the judgment of sin at Calvary.

The **sixth** dispensation is the dispensation of **grace**—the ecclesiastical period. The church is formed, and, in the latter days—the time in which we live—the church will be suddenly taken away from this earth together with the sleeping saints who come to life in the first resurrection. This is called "the secret rapture." After the saints are removed from the earth, the antichrist will appear, and there will be a great tribulation on earth. The sixth dispensation ends with the judgment of Christ's return, the destruction of the antichrist in the battle of Armageddon and the binding of Satan for a thousand years.

The **seventh** dispensation is the **Messianic period of the kingdom,** which is to be the millennial reign of Christ on earth as King of kings and Lord of lords. It is believed that in this millennial period unfulfilled Old Testament prophecies regarding Israel will be gloriously fulfilled. In a study of this seventh dispensation, we find this summary: "As to the nations and peoples of the Kingdom—the Jewish question has long been the perplexing problem of the centuries. Israel once a proverb, a byword, a curse among the nations (Zech. 8:13), now restored and converted at Christ's coming, shall be a channel of blessing and evangelization among the nations, in the Millennial Kingdom of their long rejected Messiah."[2] The seventh dispensation of the kingdom comes to an end with the resurrection of the wicked dead and their final judgment, the second death, a new heaven and a new earth and the commencement of eternity.

Israel's Restoration

According to dispensational teaching, the people of Israel will play an important role in end-time events as a bright future awaits

---

1   Philip Mauro, *The Gospel of the Kingdom, With an Examination of Modern Dispensationalism* (Boston: Hamilton Brothers, 1928), p. 28.

2   *The New "Panorama" Bible Study Course*, Victory Press Eastbourne, Sussex, Revised Edition, 1959, study 11.

the Jewish nation and God looks after His chosen people. Many seem to recognize clear signs of this already in the modern nation of Israel. The sixth dispensation, which is the period of the Christian church and the spread of the gospel to the Gentiles, is, in fact, an interruption—an interlude—in God's plan. When the church of God will have been suddenly taken from this earth and antichrist reigns for a short time, Christ will come to punish the rebellious unbelieving nations, as the cup of their iniquity shall have been filled. This will lead to the battle of Armageddon, which ends when the nations appear before the throne of the King of kings and are separated as the sheep from the goats. Those who come through this judgment will be part of the millennial kingdom, which is the dispensation of peace on earth, described by Isaiah: "The wolf and the lamb shall feed together, and the lion shall eat straw like the bullock" (Isa. 65:25). At this time, Israel, God's chosen nation, will be wholly restored and converted, and the Jewish nation will be a source of blessing and evangelism among the nations. God's kingdom will then be established in peace upon this earth.

This, in short, is the system of interpretation, known as dispensationalism, as it is taught, with some slight variations. This view of future events is becoming more and more popular.

Many people are confident that the Jewish nation will play an important role in God's final plan. Are there clear Bible passages that support this belief? Making a claim is easy, proving it beyond all question is something else. Is the anticipation of Israel's complete restoration based on a correct understanding of the Scriptures? Is the hope of all the world related to the Jewish people? Should we direct our attention towards Israel, Palestine and Jerusalem? Will God restore Israel, and, in God's providence, will they establish a glorious earthly kingdom, free from all their enemies? These are important questions that demand clear and solid biblical answers.

Did Christ Project an Earthly Kingdom?

When Jesus Christ came to this earth, what were the Jews' expectations concerning the Messiah? What would the Messiah do when He arrived? They believed that the Messiah would come to establish an earthly kingdom. Even the disciples of Jesus shared this view. They believed the Messiah would deliver them from the Roman yoke. They believed He would lead them to conquer the nations until Israel would at last become a mighty and glorious kingdom on earth.

At one point during Jesus' ministry, when Christ had fed the multitudes with only five loaves and two fishes, the Jews recognized His divine mission, and their enthusiasm swelled so much that they wanted to crown Jesus by force as their King (John 6:14, 15). Israel clearly expected an earthly kingdom with national greatness and glory. The Messiah would sit in Jerusalem on the throne of David, and all enemies would be defeated. At long last, the coming Messiah would gloriously restore Israel's dominion. It is true that God gave His chosen people many gracious promises. Yet, these promises were all clearly conditional. God said, "... *If* ye will obey my voice indeed, and keep my covenant, *then* ye shall be a peculiar treasure unto me above all people ..." (Exod. 19:5, emphasis added).

Sadly, the people of Israel did not fulfill the conditions of the promise. Time after time, they were disobedient and served other gods. As a result, when their promised Messiah came, they rejected Him. Consider what Jesus declared, ever so directly, to Pilate: "My kingdom is not of this world" (John 18:36). Jesus always spoke about the kingdom of *heaven*, not about a kingdom on earth. This was disappointing to many Jews when they realized it. Such a Messiah and kingdom were not what they wanted.

"My kingdom is not of this world." That is Christ's own clear testimony. Yet, is that what most Christians believe today? For a very large number of Christians, the messianic kingdom of Christ will be an earthly kingdom, focused on the Jewish nation. However, if Christ plainly declared that His kingdom is *not* of this world, why would we ever expect Him to establish an earthly kingdom and sit on the throne of David in Jerusalem? Is that what the Bible teaches?

If we teach that the Jews should expect a glorious kingdom on earth, then we are breathing new life into the expectations of the scribes and Pharisees during Christ's earthly ministry.

If we teach that the Jews should expect a glorious kingdom on earth, then we are breathing new life into the expectations of the scribes and Pharisees during Christ's earthly ministry. Those expectations did not result in blessing. They caused conflict and disappointment, which led to the Jewish leadership's rejection of Christ as the promised Messiah.

Cyrus I. Scofield, Promoter of Dispensationalism

But how did it come about that, in our day, new life has been breathed into the view of the scribes and Pharisees? Near the end of the nineteenth century, in the vicinity of New York, a man came to notoriety, preaching the bright earthly future of Israel. His name was Malachi Taylor. Taylor was a member of the Plymouth Brethren and a gifted preacher. It took him very little time to gather adherents who accepted his ideas about the coming of a Jewish kingdom upon this earth.

Malachi Taylor

One of those who heard him speak was Cyrus Ingerson Scofield. Scofield became convinced of Taylor's teachings and, in his enthusiasm, decided to produce a Bible with notes about the different dispensations of biblical history and the new view about the blessed future of the Jewish people. His reference Bible has, since that time, become very popular among certain groups of Christians, and the added notes have played an important role for many people. It was in this way that new life was breathed into the old Jewish, rabbinical view of an earthly kingdom anchored in the Promised Land.

But who was Scofield, and what were his background and life story?

Cyrus Ingerson Scofield, c. 1920

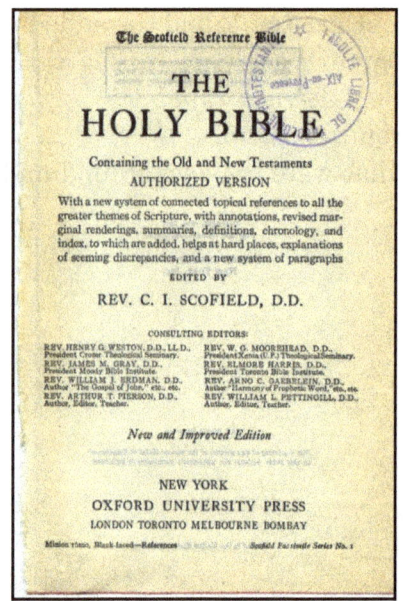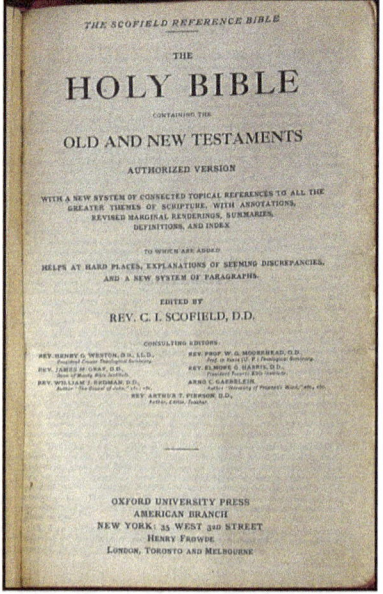

Cyrus Ingerson Scofield was born in America on August 19, 1843, in the state of Michigan.[3] He was a practicing lawyer. However, at the age of forty, he became a Christian minister and was recognized for his peculiar explanation of the Scriptures, which had its greatest acceptance within pro-Israel circles.

His thoughts and ideas, which gave influence and meaning to the teaching of dispensationalism, were added as footnotes in a Bible, published in 1909 as the *Annotated Bible*, or *Scofield Reference Bible*. It was happily received by Zionistic groups and by Israel-minded fundamentalist Christians, who have promoted dispensationalism popularly, though most Christians who favor Israel in some way would probably not know it by that name. Leading Zionists saw in Scofield's work a means to influence the Christian world to favor the establishment of the State of Israel in Palestine.

Scofield's Young Adult Life

When the American Civil War broke out, Scofield volunteered on May 20, 1861, for a year's military service with the Confederate army. He served in the Seventh Infantry of Tennessee.[4] Scofield was then almost 18 years old and too young to be admitted into the army. So, he got in by manipulating evidence that he was 21. Scofield's asserted in his application for *Who's Who in America,* vol. 7, that he was awarded the Confederate *Cross of Honor* for bravery at the Battle of Antietam.[5] There is a possibility that it was an honor given him years after the Civil War, however, none of this can be substantiated.[6] The information Scofield provided his entry in *Who's Who in America* is clearly colored in his favor with important omissions.[7] In April 1862, Scofield was registered as a patient in a hospital in Richmond, Virginia. In July 1862, he wrote a letter petitioning for discharge. He was still in the army on September 5, 1862, when his regiment crossed

---

3   "Cyrus Ingerson Scofield," available online at http://1ref.us/b6, accessed 1/24/16.

4   "Cyrus J. Scofield," in the U.S. Civil War Soldiers, 1861-1865. 7th Regiment, Tennessee Infantry, Company H, private, film M231 roll 38.

5   "Scofield, Cyrus Ingerson," *Who Was Who in America*, vol. 7 (Chicago: A. N. Marquis & Co., 1912), Albert Nelson Marquis, ed., p. 1856, available online at http://1ref.us/b7, accessed 1/24/16.

6   See "C. I. Scofield of the 7th Tennessee," available online at http://1ref.us/b8, accessed 1/24/16.

7   See the list of omissions at "The Gospel Truth: Analyzing Scofield," available online at http://1ref.us/b9, accessed 1/24/16.

the Potomac River. When his petition was finally granted, he mustered out of the army on September 26, 1862.[8]

On September 27, 1866, Scofield married Mary Leontine LeBeau Cerrè, who was from a well-known French Catholic family, in St. Louis, Missouri.[9] Leontine bore him three children: two daughters—Abigail, born on July 13, 1867, and Marie Helene, born on October 4, 1869, and a son, Guy Sylvester, who was born on January 10, 1872, but died after two short years on December 28, 1874.[10]

Scofield worked for some time in the legal office of his brother-in-law. However, he soon moved his family to Atchison, Kansas, where he ran for public office. At the age of 29, he was appointed county attorney of Kansas, and, in his oath on June 8, 1873, he swore that he had never served in combat against the United States. Once a person's life goes wrong, it often gets worse, and Scofield's life is a good example of that.

Hitting Bottom

In 1873, the very year of his appointment, Scofield withdrew from office because of several scandals: accepting bribes from railroads in public office, stealing political contributions intended for his employer Senator John J. Ingalls, and forging fraudulent notes.[11]

With sincere repentance and conversion, any of us can be assured that our sins are forgiven. However, if we continue to follow an unholy life, our sins will accuse and follow us. One of Scofield's misdeeds was serious enough to put him in the St. Louis, Missouri,

---

8   David Lutzweiler, *The Praise of Folly: The Enigmatic Life and Theology of C. I. Scofield* (Draper, VA: Apologetics Group Media, 2009), pp. 63–65. Scofield argued that he was native of Michigan, had never exercised the rights of citizenship in the Confederacy, had enlisted as a minor, was suffering from bad health, and intended to "enter Guerilla service in East Tenn." His *Who's Who in America* entry says that he served until the close of the Civil War.

9   "Missouri, Marriage Records, 1805-2002 for Cirus J Schofield [*sic*]," available online at http://1ref.us/ba, accessed 1/24/16.

10   "Mary Leontine Cerre Scofield," available online at http://1ref.us/bb, accessed 1/24/16; "Abigail Leontine Terese 'Abbie' *Scofield* Kellogg," available online at http://1ref.us/bc, accessed 1/24/16; "Helene Marie *Scofield* Barlow," available online at http://1ref.us/bd, accessed 1/24/16; "Guy Sylvester Scofield," available online at http://1ref.us/be, accessed 1/24/16.

11   One is registered as case 46333 and dated May 28, 1877, for the sum of $900, under the name of his sister, Emeline Papin; another is registered as case 44326 and dated June 28, 1877, for the amount of $250, also under his sister's name ("C. I. Scofield," http://1ref.us/bf, accessed 1/24/16; see also Department of Justice, *Bicentennial Celebration of the United States Attorneys, 1789-1989*, p. 71, available online at http://1ref.us/bg, accessed 1/28/16).

prison in 1879 for a period of six months. During this time, Christian ladies visited him, and Scofield confessed to them his faith in Christ. We wonder if this contact and his confession changed the course of his life, for, according to Scofield, it was in 1879, when he was thirty-six years old, that he converted to evangelical Christianity through the witness of a friendly lawyer, Thomas S. McPheeters, who talked seriously with Scofield about matters of faith. Was Scofield's life changed from that moment on and brought into harmony with his conversion? This is an important question that will be answered as we review subsequent events in Scofield's life.

With a lawsuit against him still pending, Scofield began working, in the fall of 1879, in public evangelism with Dwight L. Moody in St. Louis, Missouri. Since Scofield had not received a religious education, it is not clear what his duties were in Moody's campaign. Even after conversion Scofield's life was not exemplary. He was addicted to alcohol and neglected his wife and children, and there was no positive change.

According to the registry office, Scofield remained in Atchison, Kansas, from 1872 to 1873, but the following year he left, abandoning his wife and children. The gospel condemns such behavior: "But if any provide not for his own, and specially for those of his own house, he hath denied the faith, and is worse than an infidel" (1 Tim. 5:8).

In 1877, he was registered as "Scofield, Cyrus I., lawyer. Res. 3029 Dickson, St Louis, Missouri."

Even while still married, Scofield lived unrestrained and had a relationship with a young woman from the St. Louis Flower Mission. He apparently also had a relationship with Hettie Hall van Wark while he had abandoned his family without means in Atchison, Kansas.

The Old Courthouse at St. Louis, Missouri, within the middle section of the prison where Scofield was imprisoned for six months in 1879. It was here that Christian ladies visited him and had a positive influence upon him. During his imprisonment, Scofield studied the writings of John Nelson Darby, a supporter and preacher of dispensationalism.

Courthouse with prison, St. Louis, Missouri, where Scofield was imprisoned

Divorce and Remarriage

In July 1880, Scofield became a member of the *Pilgrim Congregational Church* in St. Louis. Scofield proved himself a good speaker, and the church shortly gave him a ministerial certificate and he began to preach in the *Hyde Park Congregational Church,* in St. Louis, with James H. Brookes as his mentor. Scofield served this church until the summer of 1882 when he transferred to the *First Congregational Church* of Dallas.

Part 1 A POPULAR VIEW OF ISRAEL IN PROPHECY   21

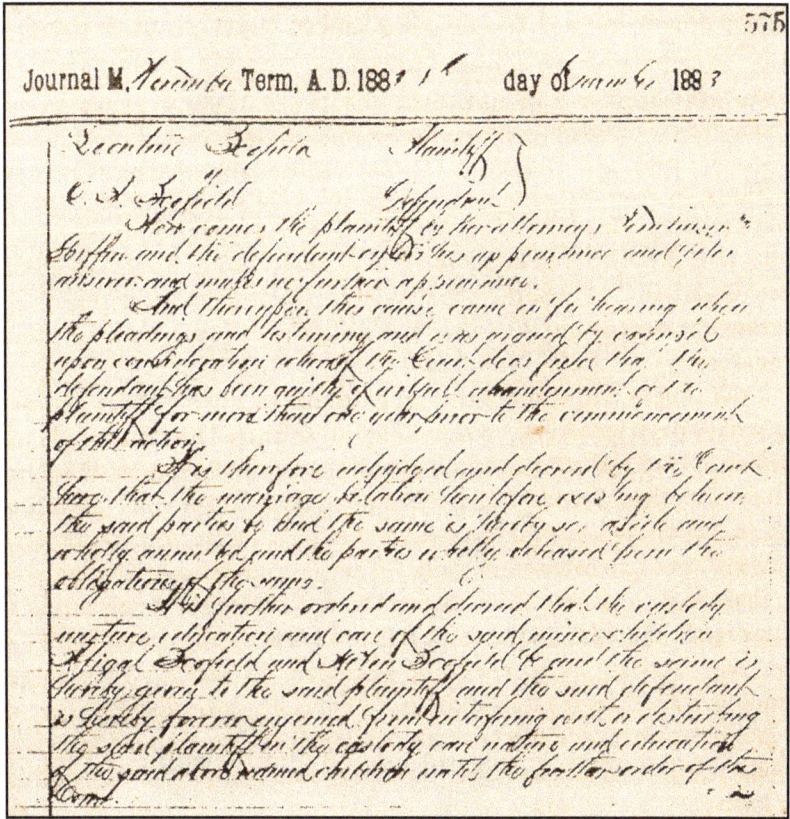

Facsimile of Scofield's Divorce Decree, 1883

On July 28, 1881, Leontine Scofield had had divorce papers drawn up, which was the same period in which Cyrus Scofield began his preaching career. She charged that he had abandoned his family and neglected his duties. He denied all charges. After a second petition in October, the divorce became final on December 8, 1883. Almost immediately after this Scofield married Hettie Hall van Wark. Remarkably, according to the date on the marriage certificate, Scofield married Hettie on March 11, 1884, though Scofield reported that they married on July 14, 1884. The later date seemingly suited him better. On December 22, 1888, Hettie bore him a son, Noël Paul.

Ordained a Minister

In October 1883, before the divorce was completed, another remarkable event took place: Scofield was ordained a Congregational minister. It is incomprehensible that this could take place while he was involved in the proceedings of a divorce from Leontine, his first wife. And if we consider the circumstances that led up to the divorce, we must admit that, on biblical grounds, Scofield was not an acceptable candidate for ordination. Scofield likely never told his congregation about his wife and daughters or that he had abandoned his family in Atchison, Kansas. It would appear that Scofield was a handy and eloquent actor when he needed to be. He could present himself better than he really was and could slant negative facts to his advantage.

By his ordination Scofield became the official minister of the *First Congregational Church* of Dallas, Texas. This church later became known as the *Scofield Memorial Church*.

Scofield learned a great deal from his mentor James H. Brookes, who pastored the *Walnut Street Presbyterian Church*, in St. Louis, and through whose friendship Darby had been influenced to become a dispensationalist. It is understandable that Brookes was a major influence on Scofield in the formation of his view of biblical prophecy.

Without Academic Training

Around 1892 Scofield began to present himself as *Reverend C. I. Scofield, D.D.*, or "Doctor of Divinity," though there is no evidence that he ever attended an institution of higher learning to obtain such a degree.

In 1895, Scofield became the minister of the *Trinitarian Congregational Church* at East Northfield, Massachusetts. After eight years there, he returned to the church in Dallas, suffering from bodily ailments. It would seem that illness from his intensive labor in preparing *The Scofield Reference Bible* and his traveling for research did not allow him much time for pastoral duties.

Scofield became a member of the prestigious *Lotus Club* of artists and writers, where he made the acquaintance of Samuel Untermyer, a Zionist and a member of the secret *Illuminati* society. Untermyer saw in Scofield's ideas a mighty weapon on behalf of Zionism and introduced Scofield to leading Jewish Zionists. They supported Scofield and had a major influence on his work.

In 1909, Scofield published his *Reference Bible*. It quickly became a powerful influence on behalf of dispensationalism and a good source of income for Scofield. During the next several years, Scofield was able to purchase property in Dallas, Texas; Ashuelot, New Hampshire; and Douglaston, Long Island. A few years after the *Reference Bible*'s publication, Scofield left the *Congregational Church* and became a member of the *Southern Presbyterian Church*, moving from

Dallas to New York City, where he became a leader of the *New York Night School of the Bible*. In 1914, he established the *Philadelphia School of the Bible,* which later became *Philadelphia Biblical University*. On July 24, 1921, Scofield died in Long Island. The memorial service was held at the *First Baptist Church* of Flushing, New York, and he was buried in the Flushing Cemetery in Queens County.

Origins of Futurism

Scofield's teachings on dispensationalism greatly resemble those of John N. Darby (1800–1882), leader of the Plymouth Brethren, a one-time lawyer. Scofield had studied the writings of Darby while in prison and became convinced of the veracity of the secret rapture and of the prophetic role of the Jews in Palestine.

Although John Darby is the father of dispensationalism, this system of biblical interpretation has earlier roots. Samuel Prideaux Tregelles and Dave MacPherson allege that Darby was, for his part, inspired by Margaret McDonald, a charismatic Christian from Glasgow, Scotland, who claimed to have had visions of a two-phased return of Christ, including a "secret rapture."[12] However, what McDonald taught was not fundamentally new. Three prominent Jesuit teachers of futurism had previously presented the core of her theological insights, including the secret rapture. These are:

Francisco Ribera (1537–1591), Jesuit priest and theologian, published a commentary on the book of Revelation in 1589/1590 and located the rapture of the church during a time period of three and a half years.

Cardinal Robert Bellarmine (1542–1621), saint and scholar, defended, in particular, the position that the prophetic days of Daniel and Revelation—1260, 1290, 2300, etc.—are actual days and not symbolic of years.

Emmanuel de Lacunza (1731–1801), a Catholic priest who defended a secret rapture of the church, published his views, based on Ribera's teaching, under the pseudonym "Rabbi Juan Josafat ben Ezra." His book, *La venida del Mesías en gloria y majestad* [The Coming of Messiah in Glory and Majesty], was first published in Spanish.

John N. Darby, Francisco Ribera, Cardinal Robert Bellarmine, Emmanuel de Lacunza

---

12 "Margaret MacDonald," available online at http://1ref.us/bh, accessed 1/26/16.

Francisco Ribera was the first to teach a two-part coming of Christ, which included Christ's coming to the earth to rapture the church first and then, afterwards, His coming to the earth to bring the final judgment. Ribera laid the foundation for futurism and the system of dispensationalism. Thus we see that the modern system of dispensationalism has its roots in the teachings of a Jesuit and of the Catholic Counter-Reformation.

Dispensationalism's Counter-Reformation Roots

The rise of the Protestant Reformation was a threat to the power of Rome. As Protestantism continued to grow steadily, many people left the Roman church and were motivated and convicted to share their new faith. Rome fought back, sowing death and ruin wherever she was threatened. Nonetheless, neither threats nor the scaffold or the stake could stop Protestantism. With Scripture as their guide, Protestants were unanimously convinced that the papacy was the antichrist and that the Roman church was the whore of Babylon. Rome employed every means available to her to halt the devastating influence of the Protestant faith upon the Roman Church. In theological circles, they eagerly sought to undermine the Protestant faith and to stifle the conviction that the pope and Catholicism were the antichrist.

Front-page of Francisco Ribera's book with futurist explanations

Francisco Ribera was the first Catholic expositor to succeed in developing a system of prophetic interpretation to counteract the identification of the papacy as the antichrist. It was the futurist explanation of the three and a half years of antichrist's reign taking place in the future. Ribera published his prophetic interpretation as a commentary on the book of Revelation, *In Sacrum Beati Ioannis Apostoli, & Evangelistiae Apocalypsin Commentarij.*

Ribera projected prophetic passages of the Bible regarding the little horn to entities of the past—heathen Rome and Antiochus Epiphanes, who is described in the book of Maccabees as profaning the Jewish temple. Other prophetic passages were projected into the future—at the end of time—when a single apostate Jew is supposed to reign as antichrist in Jerusalem.

With this exegesis, no present-day application was made, as if Bible prophecy only addresses the past and the future. The long period in between, about which the Bible would, therefore, have nothing to say, forms an interruption in Bible prophecy, which is why this explanation is called the *gap theory*. With Ribera's theory, the revelator's prophecy would be silent about the papacy's role in the Middle Ages, and Roman Catholicism would not be regarded as the biblical antichrist.

The futurist prophetic interpretation of Ribera was well received in Catholic circles. In the course of time, it received acceptance within several Protestant circles and grew into modern dispensationalism.

Biblical Interpretation with an Agenda

The purpose that Ribera had in mind with his futurist insights was to deflect the application of Bible prophecy from the papacy and Catholicism, counteracting the identification of the Roman Catholic Church as the antichrist. This was not a sincere effort to take the Bible in its most obvious sense to understand prophecy. Rather, it was exegesis, or biblical interpretation, with an agenda—to project a particular idea into the passage. The motivation for the development of futurism was solely to take away the Protestant conviction that the Catholic Church is the antichrist. The strategy has largely been successful.

The agenda for the dispensational view of prophecy, as devised by Scofield and his associates, prepared Christianity for the establishment of the state of Israel in Palestine and the special role that the Jewish nation is supposed to play in the future.

Segregated Rewards?

According to dispensational interpretation, there would be a great difference between the people of Israel in the Old Testament and the New Testament church. The Bible, on the other hand, teaches that there is no difference between Israel and the church, as we see in several verses:

> There is neither Jew nor Greek, there is neither bond nor free, there is neither male nor female: for ye are all one in Christ Jesus. And if ye *be* Christ's, then are ye Abraham's seed, and heirs according to the promise. (Gal. 3:28, 29)

> Know ye therefore that they which are of faith, the same are the children of Abraham.... So then they which be of faith are blessed with faithful Abraham.... That the blessing of Abraham might come on the Gentiles through Jesus Christ ... (Gal. 3:7, 9, 14)

> For there is no difference between the Jew and the Greek: for the same Lord over all is rich unto all that call upon him. (Rom. 10:12)

Are the faithful Gentiles blessed separately or differently from Israel? No, *they are all blessed with faithful Abraham*. The blessing of Abraham comes to the Gentiles through Christ. The apostle Paul uses the example of an olive tree as a representation of the Jewish people, and he explains that, because of unbelief, some of the branches have been broken off; and the faithful Gentiles, "being a wild olive tree, wert graffed in among them, and with them partakest of the root and fatness of the olive tree" (Rom. 11:17).

Thus, it is clear that, together with the faithful Jews, *the faithful Gentiles share the same blessings of the root and fatness of the olive tree. There is no difference*; through faith in Jesus, they are all Abraham's seed and heirs according to the promise (Eph. 3:6). Are faithful Jews and faithful Gentiles heirs of a different reward? Notice what Jesus said to the Jews regarding the faith of the Roman centurion: "And I say unto you, That many shall come from the east and west, and shall sit down with Abraham, and Isaac, and Jacob, in the kingdom of heaven" (Matt. 8:11). This clear testimony of Jesus should convince us that *faithful Jews and Gentiles are blessed together with the same reward.* Jesus spoke with the Jews a great deal about the kingdom of heaven, and nowhere did He give them any prospect of an earthly kingdom.

The Bible does not teach anywhere that the people of Israel were to have an earthly reward while the New Testament church was to have a heavenly one. Nor is there evidence in Scripture of a special period during which the Jews establish a glorious earthly kingdom and reign over the world from Jerusalem while the church has been taken up secretly into heaven. The apostle Paul establishes quite the opposite: "There is one body, and one Spirit, even as ye are called in one hope of your calling; one Lord, one faith, one baptism, one God and Father of all, who is above all, and through all, and in you all" (Eph. 4:4–6).

There is no difference. Rather, there is a *unity of body, of faith and of hope*; and there is one God and Father of all. Does the apostle here address only faithful Gentiles or perhaps only faithful Jews? Paul uses the word "all" in this passage, which precludes his addressing a particular group of believers. Moreover, just before this, in writing about the relation between Jews and Gentiles, the apostle clarified that Christ "hath made both one, and hath broken down the middle wall of partition …" (Eph. 2:14).

In harmony with this, Jesus has taught the Jews that other sheep, not of this fold (meaning, not of the Jewish fold), will also hear His voice "and there shall be one fold and one shepherd" (John 10:16).

How can it ever be said that there is only one hope, one fold, and one shepherd, if part of the fold is to be caught up into heaven and the other part is to be left on earth? That would indicate a *different* reward and a *divided* fold.

With great clarity, Jesus declared: "My kingdom is not of this world" (John 18:36). This is the reason *Abraham and all the Old Testament faithful believers were strangers and pilgrims on this earth, looking for a better, heavenly country with a city prepared by God for them* (Heb. 11:13–16). Concerning that heavenly city, Paul wrote: "Jerusalem which is above is free, which is the mother of us all," while he declared, on the other hand, the earthly Jerusalem "is in bondage with her children" (Gal. 4:25, 26).

Notice also that Old Testament and New Testament believers will not reach the fulfillment of their hopes segregated from one another but will come to their reward together. Referring to the Old

Testament worthies of faith, the author of Hebrews declares that "they without us should not be made perfect" (Heb. 11:40). The New English Bible renders this: "... that only in company with us should they reach their perfection." The Berkeley version has "... so that without us their consummation might not be attained." Thus, the Bible consistently presents a single inheritance for all believers.

In what follows, it is not my purpose to present every aspect of dispensationalism but only certain fundamental teachings that will be tested and discussed in light of Scripture. All should carefully study the Bible before accepting teachings as biblical truth. A primary teaching of dispensationalism is that the church will be suddenly caught up into the heaven.

The Secret of the Rapture

The teaching of dispensationalism is that, just before the manifestation of the antichrist and the outbreak of the great tribulation, Christ will come to take His church secretly up into heaven. Believers will meet their descending Lord in the air.

Nowhere in the Bible do we encounter the thought of the secret rapture of God's church.[13] On the contrary, what seems a "secret" to many is that the coming of Christ is described in spectacular terms. Jesus compared His coming with the **lightning** that "cometh out of the east, and **shineth** even unto the west" (Matt. 24:27). It will be a **sign, or spectacle**, at which the tribes of the earth will **mourn** as they **see** the Lord Jesus coming with **power** and **great glory** and the angels of heaven gathering God's elect from all the earth with a **great sound of a trumpet** (Matt. 24:30, 31). Paul declares that the Lord will descend with a **shout,** with the **voice** of the archangel and with the **sounding** of the **trump** of God, the **last trump**, and with it the dead in Christ will be raised in new life and, together with the faithful living, will be *caught up* to meet their Lord in the air (1 Thess. 4:16, 17; 1 Cor. 15:52). John says that everyone on earth will witness this spectacular event, for **every eye will see** Christ coming in the clouds, and **all the people of the earth will mourn and wail** (Rev. 1:7).

Scofield connected a *secret* rapture with the passages of Scripture that describe Jesus' coming as "a thief in the night" (1 Thess. 5:2;

---

13   The only mention of "secret" with reference to the Lord's return is in describing what His coming is *not:* "Wherefore if they shall say unto you, Behold, he is in the desert; go not forth: behold, *he is* in the secret chambers; believe *it* not" (Matt. 24:26).

2 Peter 3:10). Yet these passages are describing the suddenness and unexpectedness of the Lord's return. Peter describes great destruction following the Lord's sudden arrival. For those who are unprepared, Jesus will come suddenly to their destruction, as a *thief in the night*. They shall *not escape*. On the other hand, for the children of light, who are *not in darkness,* that day *will not overtake them as a thief* (1 Thess. 5:1–5).

Scofield had the antichrist appearing after the church is caught up, but is this biblical? Will the antichrist appear after Christ comes for His saints? The biblical sequence is that the antichrist comes **first** and **then** Christ will come. The apostle Paul, speaking about the coming of Christ and the gathering of His people to Him, beseeches the brethren in his days not to be soon shaken in mind, or be troubled, that the day of Christ's coming is at hand. Paul warns them emphatically: "Let no man deceive you by any means: for *that day shall not come*, except there come a falling away first, and that man of sin be revealed, the son of perdition" (2 Thess. 2:3, emphasis added). We should also note that the wicked one, who will be revealed, is to be consumed by the spirit of Christ's mouth and destroyed "with the ***brightness of His coming***" (vs. 8).

The apostle Paul presents here a convincing picture of Christ's coming, preceded by the appearance of the antichrist. With a careful reading of this passage, no one will need doubt that the antichrist is to be revealed first before Christ returns.

Not Taught by the Apostles

Scofield brought a worldwide revival to dispensationalism. He was a great promoter of the dispensational system of interpretation. His influence continues powerfully to this day. Yet, we recognize that there are many biblical objections to his teachings. Many Bible passages are in direct conflict with his futurist exegesis.

We do not find such teachings in the words of Jesus or in the writings of the apostles. The early church did not write from such a remarkable point of view. The origin of the futurism of dispensationalism came centuries later, as Jesuit scholars developed a system of prophetic explanations to counteract the Protestant Reformation.

Scofield, for his part, who in more recent times has given greater detail and impact to this teaching through the publication of his *Reference Bible*, was in his personal life a poor example of Christian consecration. He lived a frivolous life, and he did not meet the biblical requirements of a dedicated and faithful leader and teacher of the church.

"Consider ... Their Way of Life"

The Bible tells us that we should remember our leaders who have spoken the word of God to us, and we should follow their faith (Heb. 13:7). Of course, this is only applicable if they are faithful leaders, for the text counsels that we consider their life. The *New International Version* says: "Consider the outcome of their way of life and imitate their faith" (Heb. 13:7). It should be clear to everyone that if leaders are not living a faithful and dedicated life and do not meet the biblical requirements, then, of course, we are not bound to look to them as examples of faith.

Cyrus Scofield's poor example is a matter of public record. An article on Scofield's life appeared in August 1881 in the *Atchison Patriot*.[14] Atchison, Kansas, as you will recall, is the place that Scofield abandoned his first wife, Leontine. Here are some passages taken from the article:

> Cyrus I. Scofield, formerly of Kansas, late lawyer, politician and shyster generally, has come to the surface again ... The last personal knowledge that Kansans have had of this peer among scalawags, was when about four years ago, after a series of forgeries and confidence games he left the state and a destitute family and took refuge in Canada. For a time he kept under cover, nothing being heard of him until within the past two years when he turned up in St. Louis, where he had a wealthy widowed sister living who has generally come to the front and squared up Cyrus' little follies and foibles by paying good round sums of money. Within the past year, however, Cyrus committed a series of St. Louis forgeries that could not be settled so easily, and the erratic young gentleman was compelled to linger in the St. Louis jail for a period of six months.
>
> Among the many malicious acts that characterized his career was one peculiarly atrocious that has come under our personal notice. Shortly after he left Kansas, leaving

---

14   Atchison is also where Leontine is buried. The description was also carried in the Topeka *Daily Capital*, Aug. 27, 1881, and in the *Leavenworth Times*, Aug. 28, 1881, p. 7.

his wife and two children dependent upon the bounty of his wife's mother, he wrote his wife that he could invest some $1,300 of her mother's money (all she had) in a manner that would return big interest. After some correspondence he forwarded them a mortgage signed and executed by one Charles Best, purporting to convey valuable property in St. Louis. Upon this the money was sent to him. Afterward the mortgages were found to be base forgeries; no such person as Charles Best being in existence, and the property conveyed in the mortgage fictitious....

These unfavorable facts, described in this newspaper article, took place after Scofield's self-professed conversion. What are we to think of this, and what can we expect in theological reasoning from someone like him? Scofield was not only in material matters unfaithful, but he was also undependable in spiritual things. Careful research also reveals that he manipulated his interpretation of different Bible passages.

Controversial Connections

Scofield visited Westcott and Hort, two controversial scholars in London, with the intention of harmonizing his ideas as much as possible with the message of the Bible. Westcott and Hort were advocates of the error-prone Bible manuscripts of Alexandria, Egypt, and they are also known for their occultic ideas and activities. Westcott was the founder of the secret *Hermes* club, which became known for its homosexual activities. With an interest in studying spiritual phenomena, Westcott and Hort founded the *Ghost Society*, which came more and more to carry the accent of a spiritualistic séance group.

If a person has a sincere desire to present only sound biblical truth, then it is not wise to go to doubtful scholars. It is characteristic of Scofield that he made just such men his advisors.

Many faithful followers of Scofield overlook these issues and often excuse his conduct. George Bannerman Dealey, a 33rd Degree Free Mason and a member of Scofield's church and publisher of the daily *Dallas Morning News,* is one of the writers responsible for whitewashing Scofield's life to promote his work and teachings. In 1920, toward the end of Scofield's life, Charles G. Trumbull also tried to present a favorable report in his biography of Scofield entitled, *The Life Story of C. I. Scofield*. However, the witness of existing official documents cannot be expunged.

Summing Up

Besides conflicting with key teachings of the Bible, we have discovered additional aspects of the *Scofield Reference Bible* and the modern teaching of dispensationalism that make them unacceptable to sincere Christians.

Scofield was not a good example of Christian devotion, and his poor life choices cannot be overlooked in evaluating his presentation of biblical truth.

Principal among Scofield's mentors in the preparation of his *Reference Bible* were the Talmudic Jewish rabbis, who dreamed of a bright kingdom for Israel on Earth. Consequently, a large portion of the financial support and encouragement he received to publish his Bible came from Zionistic circles and secret groups from Boston, Massachusetts, known as the *Secret Six,* who had connections with the occultic *Illuminati.*

Moreover, the fundamental principles of futurism, which later grew into dispensationalism, were devised by Jesuit clergymen with a specific agenda. Thus, the foundational notion for dispensationalism was not sincere, faithful and objective Bible study, motivated by the working of God's Spirit. Neither can one overlook the occultic associations or the political influences behind dispensationalism's rise.

Part 2

*ISRAEL AND
THE NEW TESTAMENT*

Jesus and John the Baptist Announce the Kingdom of God

As we have previously noted, Jesus did not refer to an earthly kingdom in His teachings. He pointed to the spiritual character of His kingdom, declaring "the gospel of the kingdom of God, and saying, The time is fulfilled, and the kingdom of God is at hand: repent ye, and believe the gospel" (Mark 1:14, 15). Notice the two important aspects of Christ's preaching:

1. The time is fulfilled.
2. The kingdom of God is at hand.

Do these two aspects of Christ's preaching portray a future Jewish kingdom? No, Christ preached the kingdom of God, by faith and repentance, as a *present*, spiritual reality. He declared: "… behold, the kingdom of God is within you" (Luke 17:21).

Could the kingdom of God, which Jesus preached to be at hand, perhaps not in some sense also be understood as an earthly kingdom? The Bible clearly teaches that "the kingdom of God" is identical with "the kingdom of heaven," for other Bible passages make it clear that the kingdom that is at hand is the kingdom *of heaven*. "From that time Jesus began to preach, and to say, Repent: for the kingdom of heaven is at hand" (Matt. 4:17; see also Matt. 10:7). Is there a text in the Gospels that indicates that Jesus taught that the Jewish people would be in for a bright future and be restored to the Promised Land as a mighty nation? Is there a text in the Gospels that suggest that Jesus ever anticipated sitting in Jerusalem amidst the people of Israel on the throne of David? Nowhere do the Gospels provide such a text. This should give us pause. The Bible is God's holy word of truth, and every thought, theory or doctrine should be carefully tested in light of God's reliable, unfailing Word.

What message did John the Baptist preach? Did he ever describe the coming of an earthly kingdom? We read in Matthew: "In those days came John the Baptist, preaching in the wilderness of Judaea, And saying, Repent ye: for the kingdom of heaven is at hand" (Matt. 3:1, 2).

Jesus and John preached the same message. Was their message about a heavenly kingdom that was meant only for the church of the New Testament and not for the Jews? The Bible says: "Then went out to him Jerusalem, and all Judaea, and all the region round about Jordan" (Matt. 3:5). Many Pharisees and Sadducees came also to him (vs. 7). Thus, it is certain that John the Baptist preached his message, *particularly* to the Jews. John told them: "... think not to say within yourselves, We have Abraham to *our* father: for I say unto you, that God is able of these stones to raise up children unto Abraham" (vs. 9). There can be no doubt but that John preached the nearness of the kingdom of heaven *to the Jews.*

And to whom did Jesus address His message of the nearness of the heavenly kingdom? Jesus began to preach in Galilee in Capernaum, in the borders of Zabulon and the land of Nephthalim, which are the territories allotted to two of the tribes of Israel. He "... began to preach and to say, Repent: for the kingdom of heaven is at hand" (Matt. 4:17). Doubtless, Jesus also brought the message of the heavenly kingdom to the children of Israel. And what were Christ's instructions when He sent His disciples out to preach? "These twelve Jesus sent forth, and commanded them, saying, Go not into the way of the Gentiles, and into *any* city of the Samaritans enter ye not: But go rather to the lost sheep of the house of Israel" (vss. 5, 6). Thus, there is no doubt but that Jesus sent the twelve disciples exclusively to the house of Israel. And what was the special message they were to preach to the children of Israel? The next verse tells us: "And as ye go, preach, saying, The kingdom of heaven is at hand" (vs. 7). Here we plainly see that the message of the nearness of God's heavenly kingdom was preached particularly to the Jewish people. The disciples were not to go into the way of the Gentiles. Their message was only to be preached to Israel.

The Gospels provide no evidence that Israel was promised in any way an earthly kingdom of national greatness. No, Jesus spoke much about God's kingdom and about the kingdom of heaven, but He nowhere alluded that this would be an earthly kingdom in Palestine.

To consider all the Bible passages that deal with the kingdom of heaven would take a lot of time since Jesus said many things about that subject. Several of His parables are about the kingdom of heaven. What did Jesus, the Teacher sent from God, teach Israel by means of these lessons? Do they indicate that Israel will at last be restored as a people with national greatness? A careful consideration of the Gospels leads to the unequivocal conclusion that Jesus never gave the Jewish people any hope of a bright earthly kingdom in the Promised Land. The lessons Jesus taught them were of a different nature, and, unfortunately, they were not ready to accept His teaching. They held their own ideas and expectations too dear. This, of course, should come to us as no surprise. People of our time likewise prefer their own theories to the teachings of Christ.

The Fruitless Fig Tree

Not so long before Jesus made His triumphal entry into Jerusalem on a colt, He told the parable of the vineyard and the fruitless fig tree that was planted in it (Luke 13:6–8). The caretaker of the vineyard was ordered by the owner of the vineyard to cut the tree down because it had not borne fruit for three years. However, the caretaker pleaded with the owner of the vineyard to leave it be for another year. He would dig around it to aerate the roots and fertilize it, and, if the tree would remain fruitless, he would cut it down.

What is the meaning of this parable? The figure of a vineyard was familiar to the Jewish people. The prophet Isaiah had used the vineyard to symbolize the house of Israel and plants, to symbolize the men of Judah (Isa. 5:7). The fruitless fig tree, in Jesus' parable, is, therefore, a picture of Israel's barrenness—the impenitence and unfaithfulness of the men of Judah.

John the Baptist had used similar imagery in his preaching. With no mincing of words, he exhorted the people: "Bring forth therefore fruits meet for repentance ... And now also the ax is laid unto the root of the trees: therefore every tree which bringeth not forth good fruit is hewn down, and cast into the fire" (Matt. 3:8, 10). These

Part 2 ISRAEL AND THE NEW TESTAMENT

are strong words, and they leave no room for leniency. No, the decision has been made—the ax is already slicing into the tree's roots. For what purpose? Is it merely to give it a few whacks? No, no, the fruitless trees will be cut down and cast into the fire. That means that it will most definitely come to an end. Has John overstated what will happen? In His parable, Jesus did not tell what happened to the fruitless fig tree after the year's probation was over. He left that part of the story open. We assume that those in Jesus' audience, including His disciples, would have asked themselves what the end of the fig tree would be. Would it produce fruit during that last year, or would it remain barren? One can imagine the question suggested by the parable lingering in their minds. How would it go for that unfruitful tree? They did not have long to wait. Shortly after Jesus' triumphant entry into Jerusalem, He acted out an illustration that shed light on His parable. As Jesus rode on the donkey into Jerusalem, the people spread their cloaks on the road and shouted happily: "Hosanna to the son of David: Blessed *is* he that cometh in the name of the Lord; Hosanna in the highest" (Matt. 21:9). The Gospel of Luke informs us, "And when he was come near, he beheld the city, and wept over it" (Luke 19:41). The people were happy, calling out their praises to Jesus, but Jesus was sorrowful, and He wept. Why was that? The answer is in Jesus' words:

> If thou hadst known, even thou, at least in this thy day, the things *which belong* unto thy peace! but now they are hid from thine eyes. For the days shall come upon thee, that thine enemies shall cast a trench about thee, and compass thee round, and keep thee in on every side. And shall lay thee even with the ground, and thy children within thee; and they shall not leave in thee one stone upon another; because thou knewest not the time of thy visitation. (Luke 19:41–44)

Significant are Jesus' final words: "... because thou knewest not the time of thy visitation." It was the prophet Daniel who nailed down the time: "Seventy weeks are determined upon thy people and upon thy holy city, to finish the transgression ..." (Dan. 9:24). God determined a specific time that He would visit His people, but, unfortunately, they did not understand that the time of their probation was almost over.

In Jesus' parable of the unfruitful fig tree, the gardener bargained for another year to give the tree all possible care and attention he could afford. In much the same way, Christ came to His own with all compassionate attention and care. He performed many miracles in Israel, making known to them the way of life. Yet, when He entered Jerusalem triumphantly, riding on a colt, with the applause of the people, men of Judah were plotting how they could take Him captive. The leaders of Israel had chosen to reject Jesus and were filled with hatred and determination to put Him to death.

When Jesus had cleansed the temple of all undue business, He left Jerusalem and went to nearby Bethany for lodging. The next morning, as Jesus returned to the city, He was hungry and saw a fig tree full of leaves, a sure sign that the fruit season was in. Approaching the tree, He was disappointed to find no fruit on it to eat. It was an unfruitful fig tree, and Jesus spoke the significant words: "Let no fruit grow on thee henceforward for ever. And presently the fig tree withered away" (Matt. 21:19). Was the correlation of Jesus' statement with the withering of the tree happenstance? No, not at all. His words had deep meaning for those who would connect them with the parable of the unfruitful fig tree told shortly before.

A Decisive Moment

Jesus entered Jerusalem triumphantly as a King, as the prophet Zechariah had predicted: "Rejoice greatly, O daughter of Zion; shout, O daughter of Jerusalem: behold, thy King cometh unto thee: he *is* just, and having salvation; lowly, and riding upon an ass, and upon a colt the foal of an ass" (Zech. 9:9). The glorious moment of Jesus' entry into Jerusalem as king, in fulfillment of Zechariah's prophecy, was a decisive moment with official import.

But the men of Judah refused to accept Jesus and sought to kill Him. Jesus wept as He approached the city, for Israel knew not that their time of probation was nearing its end. The special care that Jesus had spent on the fruitless tree during His presence on earth was largely without success. The signs and wonders that He had performed among His people had not resulted in Israel's becoming a fruitful nation. The prophetic call, "Behold, thy King cometh unto thee," was to Israel as a nation of no effect. The Jewish leaders did all they could to temper the joy and to silence the voices. Even the sound of the children caused the leaders irritation as they shouted, "Hosanna to the Son of David." After this clear manifestation of unbelief and fruitless impenitence, Jesus pronounced His unmistakable judgment over the fruitless tree.

A Clear and Lasting Sentence

Jesus' words, "Let no fruit grow on thee henceforward for ever" and the immediate shriveling of the fig tree were not of a character to be easily passed by. Spoken by Jesus and recorded in God's holy Word, they are of great prophetic significance, and we would be wise to consider them carefully.

"Let no fruit grow on thee henceforward for ever." What did Jesus mean by these words? If the unfruitful fig tree is a picture of Israel's impenitence as a nation, then it is not difficult to understand what Jesus' words mean. Jesus made this irrevocable statement at the moment the Jewish people were filling up the measure of iniquity of their fathers by rejecting Him (Matt. 23:32), and God would soon render judgment on their fruitlessness.

The hour of decision had come, and no new time of probation was granted. The judgment was definite and immediate. The tree withered away at once. It was not a slow process. "And when the disciples saw *it*, they marvelled, saying, How soon is the fig tree withered away!" (Matt. 21:20). It would never grow fruit again. This sentence was to last forever. Such was the clear judgment Jesus spoke. Is there a way to reconcile Jesus' pronouncement with the unfruitful Jewish nation at last recovering the Promised Land and becoming a fruitful blessing to other nations? Could that ever be the meaning of Jesus' clear words? Jesus' pronouncement on the fig tree means it would never grow any fruit on it forever. When Israel is seen as symbolized by the fig tree, it is clear enough to refute any thought of a bright and fruitful recovery for the nation of Israel in Palestine.

Now, if the Jewish nation were to bear fruit during the seventh dispensation, as Scofield taught, then, Jesus would be mistaken and unreliable in His teaching, as would the message of John the Baptist. But that is not all—God's Word would be unreliable, and what safe and true foundation would we be left with to build our faith on?

It is not the Word of God but human teaching that is unreliable.

Thank God that we are not left in doubt! God's Word is absolutely certain and unfailing. It is not the Word of God but human teaching that is unreliable. And therefore we can say with absolute certainty that Israel as a nation will never again bear fruit. Nevermore will there be a moment in which the Jewish nation as a whole will be converted to God. Individually, there will undoubtedly be many Jews who will be converted as they accept Jesus Christ as their Savior. However, Israel as a nation will remain forever fruitless.

Two Sons, Two Responses

In the same chapter in Matthew, Jesus made other clear statements. Shortly after the illustrative lesson of the fruitless fig tree, Jesus responded to "the chief priests and elders" about His authority for teaching (Matt. 21:23), telling the parable of the two sons who were asked to work in their father's vineyard. The first son answered that he would not go, but later he repented and went. The second son promised to go and work in the vineyard but never did. Jesus then asked which of the two had done the will of the father?

The Jewish leaders identified, as the son who did the father's will, the son who at first refused to go, but repented and went. Receiving their answer, Jesus declared: "Verily I say unto you, That the publicans and the harlots go into the kingdom of God before you. For John came unto you in the way of righteousness, and ye believed him not: but the publicans and the harlots believed him: and ye, when ye had seen *it*, repented not afterward, that ye might believe him" (Matt. 21:31, 32).

The son that did not do the will of the father, although he had promised to do so and who did not afterward repent, is clearly the son that Jesus compared to those who rejected Him within the Jewish nation, while the other son, who refused to go, but repented and went, He compared to the harlots and publicans.

In light of this parable, is it reasonable to expect that the son who represented the Jewish rejecters of Christ will repent and be recovered at last and do the will of the father? If this is what we expect, then we demonstrate that we know more than Jesus, for He plainly stated that the first son repented not afterward. There is no hint at all that the son, who represented the rejecters of the Messiah within the Jewish nation, will repent at last and do the will of the father. Thus, in light of this parable, we are directed to believe that the recovery of Israel as a nation, in eventually doing the father's will, is only a matter of human speculation.

*Jerusalem, Old City, Tower or Citadel of King David
near the Jaffa Gate*

The Last and Best

Jesus told another relevant parable in this chapter, anticipating the end of Jewish probation. He described a certain householder, who planted a vineyard, hedged it round about, dug a winepress and built a tower and let it out unto husbandmen, or caretakers. To receive the fruits he sent his servants. However, one was beaten, another was killed and another was stoned. Again he sent servants—even more than the first time—but these also were mistreated. Then, "last of all he sent unto them his son," believing that the husbandmen would respect him (Matt. 21:37). But, no, the husbandmen recognized him to be the heir and determined to kill him so that his inheritance would be theirs. They murdered the son. Then Jesus asked His Jewish hearers: "When the lord therefore of the vineyard cometh, what will he do to these husbandmen?" (Matt. 21:33–40). They answered: "He will miserably destroy those wicked men, and will let out *his* vineyard unto other husbandmen, which shall render him the fruits in their seasons" (vs. 41). Jesus then said: "Did ye never read in the scriptures, The stone which the builders rejected, the same is become the head of the corner: this is the Lord's doing, and it is marvellous in our eyes? Therefore say I unto you, The kingdom of God shall be taken from you, and given to a nation bringing forth the fruits thereof" (vss. 42, 43). That was unmistakable, and the chief priests and Pharisees who heard the parables, "perceived that he spake of them" (vs. 45). And how did they react when they heard the sentence that the unfaithful husbandmen would be judged and the vineyard given to others? Luke says: "And when they heard *it*, they said, God forbid" (Luke 20:16). They clearly realized what was at stake, but they were not prepared to accept the lesson that Christ tried to teach them, and we read: "And the chief priests and the scribes the same hour sought to lay hands on him ... for they perceived that he had spoken this parable against them" (vs. 19).

Jesus declared unambiguously: "Therefore say I unto you, The kingdom of God shall be taken from you." Are we now entitled to say that the kingdom of God will be given back to those from whom it was taken? Will the lord of the vineyard once again put the vineyard back into the hands of unfaithful husbandmen after he has entrusted it to others? No, absolutely not! Notice that "last of all" the lord of the vineyard sent his son to these unfaithful husbandmen (Matt. 21:37). That was all that he could do. The Gospel of Mark says: "Having yet therefore one son, his wellbeloved, he sent him also last unto them..." (Mark 12:6). In doing so, the lord of the vineyard gave, as his last resort, all that he could possibly give. That was the very last act he could perform to try to bring them to repentance and collect the fruits of his vineyard.

Will the lord of the vineyard once again put the vineyard back into the hands of unfaithful husbandmen after he has entrusted it to others? No, absolutely not! Notice that "last of all" the lord of the vineyard sent his son to these unfaithful husbandmen.

We have found also that, in the parable of the fig tree, everything was done that could be done to produce fruit. The master gave one more year of probation. The dresser of the vineyard dug about the tree and fertilized it. If, after all this, there would still be no fruit, he would cut it down. In hearing the parable, the Jewish people did not know that the time of their visitation—the last allotted moments of their probation—was passing by unutilized, and they were filling up the measure of their fathers. The unmistakable message that Jesus brought to the Jewish people leaves no room to assert that there will be again a time that God will once again visit His people. The clear words of Jesus refute the view that the Jewish people will be visited with another chance. If there were another chance, then the owner's appeal through his son would not have been *last of all*. If Israel as a nation will be converted and restored to the Promised Land as God's chosen people during the millennium, then the appeal they respond to will actually be the "last." Asserting that there will be a later "last" strikes at the credibility of Christ's teaching and the reliability of God's Word.

Undeserving Wedding Guests

Continuing in the Gospels, we find that Jesus told another relevant parable. A king made a marriage for his son and sent out servants "to call them that were bidden to the wedding," but "they would not come" (Matt. 22:3). Other servants were sent forth with the message that the dinner was prepared, and they urged the guests to come to the marriage. But the guests ignored them and went their own ways, one to his farm and another to his business and others even slew some of the servants. The king, then, understandably angry, "sent forth his armies and destroyed those murderers, and burned up their city" (Matt. 22:7). Then the king said to his servants, "The wedding is ready, but they which were bidden were not worthy. Go ye therefore into the highways, and as many as ye shall find, bid to the marriage. So those servants went out into the highways, and gathered together all as many as they found, both bad and good: and the wedding was furnished with guests" (Matt. 22:8–10).

As the king arrived at the wedding feast, he noticed a guest without a wedding garment and he turned the man out into the darkness (vss. 11–13). Just being a descendant of Abraham does not, by itself, provide rights to enter God's kingdom. To attend the wedding one must have on the wedding garment, which represents the righteousness of Christ. He is the only way, truth and life. No one comes to the Father, except by Him (John 14:6).

Jesus ended the parable saying: "For many are called, but few *are* chosen" (Matt. 22:14). In other words, only a faithful remnant will be saved.

In the Gospel of Luke, the guests who were invited present all kinds of excuses for not coming. So, in their place, the poor, the maimed, the blind and the lame came in, responding to the king's invitation. Then the king in Jesus' parable emphatically points out: "For I say unto you, That none of those men which were bidden shall taste of my supper" (Luke 14:24). This means that, even if the guests who were invited call themselves children of Abraham, they will not taste of the supper. The Gospel of Matthew adds that the Pharisees "took counsel how they might entangle Jesus in his talk" (Matt. 22:15). Apparently, they recognized that Jesus had spoken about them again. That Jesus, in His teaching, was indeed addressing the Jewish people is affirmed when He said shortly afterwards: "O Jerusalem, Jerusalem, *thou* that killest the prophets, and stonest them which are sent unto thee, how often would I have gathered thy children together, even as a hen gathereth her chickens under *her* wings, and ye would not!" (Matt. 23:37).

The Jewish people—the children of Jerusalem—were the bidden guests. Yet, they would not come. It was they who slew the servants sent to them. And, as Jesus related in the parable, the king became angry and sent forth his armies to destroy those who murdered his servants, and he burned up their city. In 70 AD, the Roman armies came to Jerusalem and killed many Jews while the city burned down. Jesus finished the parable saying that the wedding was ready, yet those who were invited were not worthy. Therefore, others were invited to fill the place of gathering The kingdom was taken away from the original invitees and given to others.

Does this parable teach that the Jewish people were called to an earthly kingdom? Is the wedding to which they were invited on this earth? In introducing the parable, Jesus told the Jews: "The kingdom of heaven is like unto a certain king, which made a marriage for his son" (Matt. 22:2). Since the parable is about the "kingdom of *heaven*," it tells us that it is a heavenly kingdom into which the guests were invited to the wedding. However, as Jesus told them, those who refused to come were not worthy. Someone may say: *But wait a moment—later on they will be ready. Let us be patient and we will see that they will indeed come. God is at work with them now. He will invite them once again into an earthly kingdom in Palestine—not a heavenly one—where they will enter and share the blessings of the wedding.* Is this what Jesus taught? If we believe and preach such things, then we know more than Jesus ever has made clear. But more than that, it is clearly in conflict with Jesus' words and with God's holy Word. If Jesus declared that His kingdom is not of this world, how can He then ever establish an earthly kingdom with the Jews?

If Jesus declared that His kingdom is not of this world, how can He then ever establish an earthly kingdom with the Jews?

Jesus declared that the kingdom was to be taken from them and given to another nation that will bring forth the fruits thereof (Matt. 21:43). How can Jesus then ever come and give them the kingdom back when it is taken away from them and while it has been given to others?

Jesus has plainly taught, as He did in the parable of the fruitless fig tree, that the Jewish nation had received their last chance to bring forth fruit. One more year of probation was granted, and, if Israel still did not produce the fruit of repentance, they would be cut down. That is a definite end. How then will it be possible for God, in the last days, to visit them again with a bright future of national greatness? Jesus' teaching is that it would never grow any fruit on it again forever. Jesus repeated this same testimony in different ways, and never did He indicate that there would eventually be a complete turnabout. Thus, there is no reason to expect that the Jewish nation as a whole will ever be converted. Those who believe this, mislead themselves and do not possess the truth as it is in Christ Jesus.

When "My House" Became "Your House"

Jesus spoke strong words as He addressed the leaders of Israel: "But woe unto you, scribes and Pharisees, hypocrites! for ye shut up the kingdom of heaven against men: for ye neither go in *yourselves*, neither suffer ye them that are entering to go in" (Matt. 23:13).

Notice that Jesus speaks about the kingdom of heaven being shut up by Israel's leaders. There are, however, faithful ones who are entering the kingdom of heaven, but such ones have often been held back by their leaders. It is God's desire and purpose that the Jews enter the heavenly kingdom. However, as a whole, they have been unwilling, unfruitful and unrepentant. Israel's leaders were more of a curse than a blessing to the people. Of them, Jesus said: "Woe unto you, scribes and Pharisees, hypocrites! for ye compass sea and land to make one proselyte, and when he is made, ye make him twofold more the child of hell than yourselves" (vs. 15). These words of Jesus are very strong, and, as we read the whole chapter, we notice that He has spoken many strong words, blaming the leaders for filling up the measure of their fathers (vs. 32). Finally Jesus said: "Behold, your house is left unto you desolate" (vs. 38).

Jesus had spoken about the temple as "my house" and as "my Father's house" (Matt. 21:12, 13; John 2:16). In the end, however, He no longer calls it His or His Father's house but "*your* house." "*Your* house," He said, "is left unto you desolate." Their impenitence was great. The beloved and only Son of the Lord of the vineyard, who was sent to appeal to the husbandmen *last of all*, was openly rejected, and Israel's leaders sought to kill Him. Israel as a nation severed the tie that connected them to God. "Your house is left unto you desolate"—such sad words! God withdrew Himself from His people. God would no longer look after Jerusalem, her children and her beautiful temple. When they rejected His Son, He rejected them. Under divine inspiration, Moses had prophesied in song many years before that this would occur: "You deserted the Rock, who fathered you; you forgot the God who gave you birth. The LORD saw this and rejected them because he was angered by his sons and daughters. 'I will hide my face from them,' he said, 'and see what their end will be …' " (Deut. 32:18–20, NIV). Christ was the Rock who accompanied His people (1 Cor. 10:4), but, sadly, they deserted Him. Therefore, God rejected them and has hidden His face from them, leaving them to the consequences that resulted from their own choice. How can one ever construe this to mean that, in the end, they will be a restored, blessed nation, ruling the earth triumphantly with Christ as their King on David's throne? If that is ever the case, then the inspired prophetic words spoken by Moses will be turned into a false prophecy and the words of Jesus, condemned as a mistake.

Old Street in the historical part of Jerusalem

Children of the Flesh Vs. Children of the Promise

The apostle John wrote that Christ, the Word, came to His own, but His own received Him not (John 1:11). Then follows a statement of hope: "But as many as received him, to them gave he power to become the sons of God, *even* to them that believe on his name: Which were born, not of blood, nor of the will of the flesh, nor of the will of man, but of God" (John 1:12, 13).

Only those who accept Christ in faith, receiving power to become the sons of God, are born of God—not the fleshly children of Abraham's bloodline. Only those who receive Christ in faith are the children of God. They are God's elect. The Scriptures make clear that being a descendant of Abraham does not qualify. No, what matters is being born of God.

> *The Scriptures make clear that being a descendant of Abraham does not qualify. No, what matters is being born of God.*

God once called the Jewish nation to be His people. They were the children of God. The apostle Paul says, "... my brothers, those of my own race, the people of Israel. Theirs is the adoption as sons ..." (Rom. 9:3, 4, NIV). The Israelites were made God's sons, but were they born of God?[15] The Bible says that the Lord was angered by His sons and daughters, for they did not receive His only Son when He came to His own. The apostle Paul explains: "For they *are* not all Israel, which are of Israel: Neither, because they are the seed of Abraham *are they* all children: but, In Isaac shall thy seed be called. That is, They which are the children of the flesh, these *are* not the children of God: but the children of the promise are counted for the seed" (Rom. 9:6–8). The important question now is: Who are the children of the promise? How are they identified in the Scriptures? The answer comes in Paul's epistle to the Galatians, where we read: "Now we, brethren, as Isaac was, are the children of promise" (Gal. 4:28). It should be noted that Isaac was born in a supernatural way. His mother, Sarah, had passed the

---

15 On the day of Pentecost, many thousands of Jews did receive the Messiah and were born again (Acts 2:41). The greatest part of the very early church was Jewish.

time when she could naturally bear a child. No wonder Sarah laughed! She could not believe that, as old as she was, she would have a child (Gen. 18:13), yet God expected her to demonstrate faith in His power. Abraham's faith, however, was not weakened in spite of his own age and "the deadness of Sarah's womb" (Rom. 4:19).

Thus, the children of the promise, who are compared with Isaac, should also be born by faith in a supernatural way—they should be born of God. The apostle John indicates that only those who are born of God are God's children, and he makes clear that this birth is not "according to the flesh." Natural descent, therefore, does not count.

In light of what the Bible teaches, is it legitimate to assert that the Jews, according to the flesh, are God's children? No, absolutely not. Only those who are by faith—those who are born of God—are His children. To be born of God is what matters.

A Nighttime Visit

In the still of the night, a Pharisee named Nicodemus, who was a ruler of the Jews, came to Jesus, greeting Him with expressions of faith that Jesus was a teacher sent from God. Jesus abruptly responded: "Verily, verily, I say unto thee, Except a man be born again, he cannot see the kingdom of God" (John 3:3). Nicodemus did not understand what Jesus meant. He thought only in literal terms of a natural birth, and he asked: "How can a man be born when he is old? can he enter the second time into his mother's womb, and be born?" (vs. 4). Nicodemus was a Jew, and the Jews always emphasized their fleshly origin (cf. Matt. 3:9; Luke 3:8). They were the children of Abraham; they believed that the kingdom of God was given to them. Nicodemus was puzzled by Jesus' statement about being "born again." *How can children of Abraham be born again?* he thought. His Jewish way of thinking stood in the way of his understanding what Jesus meant.

But, you know, this old Jewish view has become very popular again. Many people today think like Nicodemus, in terms of Israel "after the flesh" (1 Cor. 10:18; Gal. 4:23, 29). They believe that the Jews are God's chosen people. They believe that the children of Abraham are in for a bright future. They believe that Israel "after the flesh" are God's elect and that, as a restored nation, they will play a leading role in Palestine, the Promised Land.

Unfortunately, many people have not paid much attention to the valuable teaching of Jesus, the Teacher sent by God. As a result, they are misled by unbiblical theories.

Jesus said that no one can see the kingdom of God unless he is born again. What good is it for a man to be a descendant of Abraham without being born again? Consider John the Baptist's message: "Bring forth therefore fruits meet for repentance: And think not to say within yourselves, We have Abraham to *our* father ..." (Matt. 3:8, 9). Consider also what Jesus said when the Jews answered: "We be Abraham's seed ... Abraham is our father ..." (John 8:33, 39). Jesus said: "If ye were Abraham's children, ye would do the works of Abraham" (vs. 39).

Unfortunately, their works were not those of Abraham, and Jesus addressed them plainly: "Ye are of your father the devil ..." (vs. 44). Jesus established that only those who do the works of Abraham and follow his faithful example are his children. Not of blood, not according to fleshly descent—no, the only thing that matters is if one does Abraham's works, bears the fruit of faith and is born again. Then only is someone "Abraham's seed," and this applies to everybody alike without any difference. Jesus did not say to Nicodemus, Except a Jew be born again, or except a Gentile be born again. Jesus said: "Except a man be born again ..." (John 3:3). This includes every person, regardless of gender and nationality. The blessing of God's kingdom is not reserved for a special nation. Jesus continued: "Verily, verily, I say unto thee, Except a man be born of water and *of* the Spirit, he cannot enter into the kingdom of God" (John 3:5). Being born of water and of the Spirit is, for every person alike, the condition for entering God's kingdom. Jesus used the word "whosoever" in saying, "... that whosoever believeth in him should not perish, but have eternal life" (vs. 15), and a second time in saying, "For God so loved the world, that he gave his only begotten Son, that whosoever believeth in him should not perish, but have everlasting life" (vs. 16). The love of God is for all people upon the earth. No one is particularly privileged above all others. The blessings of God's kingdom apply to everyone alike on condition of being born again.

The blessings of God's kingdom apply to everyone alike on condition of being born again.

Jesus told Nicodemus the truth he should know. Jesus did not say a word about an earthly kingdom in the future for the nation of Israel. He explained to Nicodemus that, for all people alike, there is only one way to be saved, to have everlasting life. It is by being born of the Spirit. Natural Israel "after the flesh" could never see nor enter God's kingdom. A natural Israelite can only be saved by bearing fruit, by being born a spiritual Israelite through faith in Jesus. There is no other way for anyone to be saved, not for the Jews, not for the Gentiles.

The End of Jewish Segregation

If there is only one way for all people alike to be saved, then it follows that there is no difference between Jews and Gentiles, and that is precisely what Jesus and the apostles proclaimed.

Prior to hearing the gospel, the Gentiles were "without Christ, being aliens from the commonwealth of Israel, and strangers from the covenants of promise, having no hope, and without God in the world" (Eph. 2:12). This was not because God did not love the Gentiles, but, rather, because they had chosen to follow their own way. If a Gentile demonstrated faith in the God of Israel, he would be accepted without any difference. When the Israelites left Egypt on the way to the Promised Land, a number of Egyptians, who apparently had decided to serve the God of Israel, went with them. Moses recollected: "And a mixed multitude went up also with them ..." (Exod. 12:38). There was to be no difference between the Israelites and the strangers that lived among them. "One law shall be to him that is homeborn, and unto the stranger that sojourneth among you" (vs. 49). God did not build a dividing wall between the Israelites and strangers, between the Jews and the Gentiles who joined themselves to the Lord (Isaiah 56:6). There is no partiality with God (Deut. 10:17).

Ellen G. White, a truly devoted woman, who lived daily in close communion with God, wrote in one of her remarkable books:

> The opinion is held by many that God placed a separating wall between the Hebrews and the outside world; that His care and love, withdrawn to a great extent from the rest of mankind, were centered upon Israel. But God did not design that His people should build up a wall of partition between themselves and their fellow men. The heart of Infinite Love was reaching out toward all the inhabitants of the earth. Though they had rejected Him, He was con-

stantly seeking to reveal Himself to them and make them partakers of His love and grace. His blessing was granted to the chosen people, that they might bless others.

God called Abraham, and prospered and honored him; and the patriarch's fidelity was a light to the people in all the countries of his sojourn. Abraham did not shut himself away from the people around him. He maintained friendly relations with the kings of the surrounding nations, by some of whom he was treated with great respect; and his integrity and unselfishness, his valor and benevolence, were representing the character of God. In Mesopotamia, in Canaan, in Egypt, and even to the inhabitants of Sodom, the God of heaven was revealed through His representative....

God called Israel, and blessed and exalted them, not that by obedience to His law they alone might receive His favor and become the exclusive recipients of His blessings, but in order to reveal Himself through them to all the inhabitants of the earth. It was for the accomplishment of this very purpose that He commanded them to keep themselves distinct from the idolatrous nations around them.[16]

It was the Jews who had built a dividing wall between themselves and others, and Christ came to break it down: "For he is our peace, who hath made both one, and hath broken down the middle wall of partition *between us;* ... And that he might reconcile both unto God in one body by the cross, having slain the enmity thereby: and came and preached peace to you which were afar off, and to them that were nigh" (Eph. 2:14, 16, 17). Thus, in Christ, all division is taken away. "For through him we both have access by one Spirit unto the Father. Now therefore ye are no more strangers and foreigners, but fellowcitizens with the saints, and of the household of God; and are built upon the foundation of the apostles and prophets, Jesus Christ himself being the chief corner *stone*: In whom all the building fitly framed together groweth unto an holy temple in the Lord: In whom ye also are builded together for an habitation of God through the Spirit" (vss. 18–22).

Can we, in light of these clear words, still proclaim that Israel "after the flesh," are God's chosen people? If there is no division between

---

16   Ellen G. White, *Patriarchs and Prophets* (Washington, DC: Review & Herald Publ. Assn., 1890, 1958), pp. 368, 369.

Jews and Gentiles, can we then expect that God will be particularly jealous of the Jews, returning to them with great mercies and establishing them in Palestine as a blessed and prosperous nation with Jesus as their King? If that would be so, then there is still a division between Jews and Gentiles and the separation wall—the segregating wall—is not broken down but a great deal of it is still standing. And how then can Jews and Gentiles be fitly framed together to become a holy temple with such a divide?

If it were true that the apostles and prophets had a different future in mind for Israel and the Gentiles, then the Gentile believers could not be perfectly built together with Israel as fellow-citizens upon the same foundation, for each would have a different reward. The Bible says: "*There is* one body, and one Spirit, even as ye are called in one hope of your calling; one Lord, one faith, one baptism, One God and Father of all, who *is* above all, and through all, and in you all" (Eph. 4:4–6). So there is unity and not division, and, therefore, it is impossible that the Jewish people should have a special and different hope of national prosperity. Paul affirms this: "For there is no difference between the Jew and the Greek: for the same Lord over all is rich unto all that call upon him" (Rom. 10:12). "*No difference!*" he said. Not an earthly kingdom for one and a heavenly kingdom for the other. The same Lord is Lord of all and rich unto all. He is not for the Jew in a different way than He is for the Greek. He is not a little richer for the one than for the other. Can we still proclaim that He blesses the one with a special blessing because he is a Jew, and the other with another blessing because he is a Greek?

The same Lord is Lord of all and rich unto all. He is not for the Jew in a different way than He is for the Greek. He is not a little richer for the one than for the other.

A Different Blessing for Jews and Gentiles?

Does the blessing of Abraham apply to Israel and the blessing of faith to the Gentiles? Many people believe that Israel occupies a special position in God's plan. God has committed himself to Abraham and his posterity, and the blessing of Abraham remains for his offspring up to a thousand generations. The Lord God of Israel will always remember His covenant with Abraham. That which God has promised He will always fulfill. Will the Jew then receive the blessing of Abraham and the Gentile the blessing of faith?

The apostle Paul gives us a clear answer: "So then they which be of faith are blessed with faithful Abraham" (Gal. 3:9). The *New English Bible* says: "Thus it is the men of faith who share the blessing with faithful Abraham." Are the faithful Gentiles blessed apart from the Jews? No, the Bible clearly says that they are blessed with Abraham; they share with Abraham the same blessing. Thus, there is no difference in blessing, as Paul declares: "That the blessing of Abraham might come on the Gentiles through Jesus Christ ..." (Gal. 3:14). The *New English Bible* says: "... that the blessing of Abraham should in Jesus Christ be extended to the Gentiles ..." The *New International Version* has it this way: "He redeemed us in order that the blessing given to Abraham might come to the Gentiles ..."

The apostle Paul explains in another letter: "In former generations this was not disclosed to the human race; but now it has been revealed by inspiration to his dedicated apostles and prophets, that through the Gospel the Gentiles are joint heirs with the Jews, part of the same body, sharers together in the promise made in Christ Jesus" (Eph. 3:5, 6, NEB). This clearly indicates that, in Christ, all previous differences between faithful Jews and faithful Gentiles are completely taken away. Although the Jews as a nation failed to be obedient and rejected their Messiah, no one need doubt that the faithful remnant of the Jews and the faithful Gentiles are together on the same plane, as one body, and they receive the same blessing—the blessing of Abraham. There is no difference; believing Jews and believing Greeks, or Gentiles, are not to remain apart from one another; they form one body. Faithful Jews and Gentiles receive the same blessing and the same promise, so there cannot be a difference in destination either. They are joint heirs of the same kingdom.

Thus we read Jesus' description of the joint reward: "... many shall come from the east and west, and shall sit down with Abraham, and Isaac, and Jacob, in the kingdom of heaven" (Matt. 8:11). Abraham believed God and so does the Gentile believer.

The apostle Paul wrote: "Even as Abraham believed God, and it was accounted to him for righteousness. Know ye therefore that they which are of faith, the same are the children of Abraham" (Gal. 3:6, 7). It is clear enough that the children of faith, and not the children of the flesh, are Abraham's children.

God knew beforehand that the Jewish nation would not accept the Rock, Jesus Christ, as their Messiah. His own sons and daughters provoked Him, and He swore to them that He would reject them (Deut. 32:18, 19, NIV). He knew that they would not be obedient and faithful, but that they would fill up the measure of iniquity of the fathers. When they did, He took His kingdom away from them and gave it to another nation that would bring forth the fruits of faith (Matt. 23:32; 21:43). In harmony with Jesus' teaching, the apostle Paul declared: "And the scripture, foreseeing that God would justify the heathen through faith, preached before the gospel unto Abraham, *saying*, In thee shall all nations be blessed. So then they which be of faith are blessed with faithful Abraham" (Gal. 3:8, 9).

Thus, it was always God's plan that faithful Gentiles become children of Abraham through Christ. Together with the faithful remnant of Israel, they are the children of the promise, fellow-citizens of the household of God. As such, we are assured: "For ye are all the children of God by faith in Christ Jesus.... There is neither Jew nor Greek ... for ye are all one in Christ Jesus. And if ye be Christ's, then are ye Abraham's seed, and heirs according to the promise" (vss. 26, 28, 29). If the Bible repeats several times, in clear, plain and straightforward statements, that all believers—without any national difference—are children of Abraham in Christ, then why should we focus our attention on the Jewish nation of Israel and on Jerusalem in Palestine? Is part of the partition wall still standing because special promises for Israel remain to be fulfilled?

Part 2 ISRAEL AND THE NEW TESTAMENT 57

Jerusalem, Greek Orthodox Church and Monastery of St Stephen in the Kidron Valley

A People in Bondage

The apostle Paul, speaking about the two sons of Abraham, points out that one of Abraham's sons was born of Hagar, his slave or bondmaid, and that the other was born of Sarah, his freeborn wife. Ishmael, the son of the bondmaid, was born "after the flesh," while Isaac, the other son of his free wife, was born through God's promise. Paul signals that the two women stand for two covenants. Hagar, the bondwoman bearing children into slavery, compares with the Sinai covenant. The Arabic name for Sinai resembles the name "Hagar," and Paul concludes: "Now Hagar stands for Mount Sinai in Arabia and corresponds to the present city of Jerusalem, because she is in slavery with her children" (Gal. 4:25, NIV).

Jesus wept over Jerusalem, for they did not know the way of peace; they did not know God's time of visitation (Luke 19:41, 42, 44). And Jesus had spoken a sevenfold *woe* (Matt. 23:13–29) to Jerusalem's leaders, His wayward children, lamenting: "O Jerusalem, Jerusalem, *thou* that killest the prophets, and stonest them which are sent unto thee, how often would I have gathered thy children together, even as a hen gathereth her chickens under *her* wings, and ye would not! Behold, your house is left unto you desolate" (Matt. 23:37, 38). Jesus would have gathered Jerusalem's children, but they would not come. Consequently, He disowned His house and said, "*Your* house is left *unto you* desolate." There is no promise that Jesus will accept their house again and restore it. No, it is left unto them desolate. "Jerusalem," Paul wrote, "is in slavery with her children."

How wise is it then to direct all our interest and energy into a city and a people in slavery, expecting that, in the time of the end, wonderful things will happen there and Old Jerusalem will be accepted, rebuilt and established by God?

Ellen G. White wisely counseled:

> I was pointed to some who are in the great error of believing that it is their duty to go to Old Jerusalem and think they have a work to do there before the Lord comes. Such a view is calculated to take the mind and interest from the present work of the Lord ... I saw that such a mission would accomplish no real good, that it would take a long while to make a very few of the Jews believe even in the first advent of Christ, much more to believe in His second advent ...

I also saw that Old Jerusalem never would be built up; and that Satan was doing his utmost to lead the minds of the children of the Lord into these things now, in the gathering time, to keep them from throwing their whole interest into the present work of the Lord, and to cause them to neglect the necessary preparation for the day of the Lord.[17]

We should focus our attention on the free heavenly Jerusalem. As Paul said, "But Jerusalem which is above is free, which is the mother of us all" (Gal. 4:26). What a striking contrast—bondage versus freedom! Jerusalem above is the mother of the children of promise. Therefore, the heavenly city should have our interest—not the earthly Jerusalem.

Jerusalem above is the mother of the children of promise. Therefore, the heavenly city should have our interest— not the earthly Jerusalem.

The ones to whom the apostle Paul directed his letter were mostly believers of Gentile origin. To them he wrote: "Now we, brethren, as Isaac was, are the children of promise" (vs. 28). Does God still have bright promises in store, apart from Christ, for the children of Jerusalem in Palestine—the city that corresponds to Hagar, the bondwoman? Consider what the Scripture says: "Cast out the bondwoman and her son: for the son of the bondwoman shall not be heir with the son of the freewoman" (vs. 30). Could it be any clearer? Earthly Jerusalem with her children are not heirs. No, they will be sent away. They will be cast out. The promises do not apply to earthly Jerusalem. The *New International Version* says: "Get rid of the slave woman and her son, for the slave woman's son will never share in the inheritance with the free woman's son." Then the apostle concludes: "So then, brethren, we are not children of the bondwoman, but of the free" (vs. 31). This is the clear, straightforward testimony of the Bible. This represents a great shift. The promises to Israel were all given on condition of faith and obedience. When the Jewish nation proved unfaithful and disobe-

---

17   Ellen G. White, *Early Writings* (Washington, DC: Review & Herald Publ. Assn., 1882, 1945), pp. 75, 76.

dient and even killed her Messiah, the kingdom was taken from them and given to another nation.

Should we not have confidence in God's clear and unfailing holy Word? Or should we join with human philosophies in supporting an earthly Jewish kingdom, as popularly taught in some Christian circles? The Bible has predicted that, in the time of the end, there will be false teachers and prophets and that they shall deceive many (Matt. 24:11, 24; 1 John 4:1). For this reason, we should be extremely cautious. The apostle Paul predicted that the time will come when people will not want to hear sound doctrine but, rather, will gather around them teachers who will say the things they want to hear (2 Tim. 4:3), producing great confusion. This is all the more reason that we should carefully study the Bible for ourselves before accepting any popular teaching. All are free to make their own choice about what to believe, but why not make it a good, solid, and biblically based choice? Let us keep our eyes always fixed upon the heavenly Jerusalem, for she is the mother of us all.

All are free to make their own choice about what to believe, but why not make it a good, solid, and biblically based choice?

Desiring a Heavenly Country

The faithful witnesses of old, say the Scriptures, were looking for a country. Yet, God called Abraham to leave his home and travel to a land that he and his heirs should receive for an inheritance. The apostle Paul observes: "By faith he sojourned in the land of promise, as *in* a strange country, dwelling in tabernacles with Isaac and Jacob, the heirs with him of the same promise" (Heb. 11:9).

And they all died in faith without having received the promise, confessing that they were strangers and pilgrims on the earth. The apostle Paul explains: "But now they desire a better *country*, that is, an heavenly: wherefore God is not ashamed to be called their God: for he hath prepared for them a city" (Heb. 11:16).

Were the faithful believers of old looking for an earthly kingdom or city? No, they desired a better, *heavenly* country, and God had prepared a city for them. It was "a city which had foundations, whose builder and maker *is* God" (vs. 10). Thus, the faithful witnesses of old had a hope built in God's heavenly kingdom, whose capital city, prepared for them by God, is the New Jerusalem.

Is the heavenly kingdom reserved for the New Testament church but an earthly kingdom with an earthly city for the Jewish nation of Israel? No, the Bible says, the faithful believers of old were longing for a better, *heavenly* country, and they were looking for the city that is built by God. The land of their dreams was not an earthly country but the heavenly kingdom with its capital, the New Jerusalem. The faithful believers of old knew what they believed and what they were looking for.

With reference to the centurion's faith, Jesus told the people who followed Him: "Verily I say unto you, I have not found so great faith, no, not in Israel. And I say unto you, That many shall come from the east and west, and shall sit down with Abraham, and Isaac, and Jacob, in the kingdom of heaven. But the children of the kingdom shall be cast out ..." (Matt. 8:10–12). Why is it that the children of the kingdom will be cast out? It will be because they do not reveal the faith of their father Abraham, whose hope was fixed upon a heavenly country and the New Jerusalem. They are cast out because they were only dreaming of an earthly kingdom with national prosperity. The only way they would have accepted the Messiah is if He had satisfied their earthly hopes and expectations.

And how is it with us in our day? Do we have Abraham's faith, or do we go along with Israel's children who are in bondage and who dream of a bright national state in Palestine?

The family of Old Testament believers will join with the family of New Testament believers in God's heavenly kingdom. At the coming of Christ, they will all jointly receive their final reward.

Christ said plainly that His kingdom is not of this world. Christ, the apostles and John the Baptist preached the arrival of a heavenly kingdom, which the faithful witnesses of old anticipated as the object of their promised hope. These witnesses all died without having received the fulfillment of the promise. Nonetheless, God's plan is for Gentile believers to enjoy the company of these faithful believers in perfection (Heb. 11:40). There is not the least shadow of division or segregation anticipated. The family of Old Testament believers will join with the family of New Testament believers in God's heavenly kingdom. At the coming of Christ, they will all jointly receive their final reward.

The Jews were familiar with the idea that they were, as children of Israel, the sheep of God's pasture (Ezek. 34:30, 31; Ps. 74:1; 95:7; 100:3). Jesus described for the Jews the future influx of non-Jews as "other sheep," not of their fold: "But there are other sheep of mine, not belonging to this fold, whom I must bring in; and they too will listen to my voice. There will then be one flock, one shepherd" (John 10:16, NEB).

The apostle Paul illustrated the reality of the union of believing non-Jews with believing Jews through the emblem of the olive tree. The unfaithful branches had been broken off, and faithful Gentile branches had been grafted in among the true branches of Israel. As the full number of believing Gentile branches are brought in, only faithful Jewish and faithful Gentile branches will remain connected to the olive tree. The apostle concludes by saying, "And so all Israel shall be saved" (Rom. 11:26). By this he means that all faithful Jews and all faithful Gentiles will then jointly, as one fold and as all Israel, attain their final consummation, their final reward.

A Divine Revelation Pronounces Gentiles Clean

It was a surprising revelation for the Jewish believers that the Gentile believers were also called by God as Abraham's children. Even the apostle Peter had problems with it at first. Yet, through the vision of something that looked like a great sheet descending from heaven with all kinds of clean and unclean creatures in it, he recognized that he should not call any person "unclean."

At the same time, Cornelius, a devout centurion who feared God with all his house, also had a vision. An angel addressed him, telling him to send to Joppa for a man called "Simon Peter" who lodged with a tanner in a house by the sea. When the three men sent by Cornelius arrived, Peter was even then troubled over what the vision could mean. Luke tells the story: "While Peter thought on the vision, the Spirit said unto him, Behold, three men seek thee. Arise therefore, and get thee down, and go with them, doubting nothing: for I have sent them" (Acts 10:19, 20). When Peter met up with Cornelius in Caesarea with Cornelius's relatives and close friends, he said: "I need not tell you that a Jew is forbidden by his religion to visit or associate with a man of another race; yet God has shown me clearly that I must not call any man profane or unclean. That is why I came here without demur when you sent for me" (vss. 28, 29, NEB). Thus, Peter demonstrated that he had allowed his Jewish prejudice born of traditional Pharisaism to be overruled by the vision that God gave him. After Cornelius related his wonderful experience, Peter confessed: "I now see how true it is that God has no favorites, but that in every nation the man who is god-fearing and does what is right is acceptable to him" (vss. 34, 35, NEB). Peter then preached to them Jesus Christ, told of the good works Christ had done and that He had been sent by God, to whom all the biblical prophets testify. While still speaking, the Holy Spirit came upon all who heard the message, and they spoke in other tongues and magnified God. The Jewish believers, who accompanied Peter, were much astonished that the gift of the Holy Spirit was also poured out on the Gentiles (vss. 44–46).

"Then Peter said, 'Can anyone keep these people from being baptized with water? They have received the Holy Spirit just as we have.' So he ordered that they be baptized in the name of Jesus Christ" (vss. 46–48, NIV).

Thus, once again, we clearly see that with God there is no difference between believing Jews and Gentiles. God gave the Holy Spirit to them the same way. When, later on, some of the believing Jews, who were of the opinion that believing Gentiles should be circumcised, criticized Peter for lodging with uncircumcised men, Peter rehearsed the whole story and explained that the Holy Spirit came upon these Gentiles just as He had come upon the believing Jews (Acts 11:15). Peter told them: "Then I recalled what the Lord had said: 'John baptized with water, but you will be baptized with the Holy Spirit.' God gave them no less a gift than he gave us when we put our trust in the Lord Jesus Christ; then how could I possibly stand in God's way?" (vss. 16, 17, NEB). Peter's clear testimony is that it is the Lord's doing that all those who trust in Christ Jesus will receive the same gift of the Holy Spirit—Jews and Gentiles alike—without any difference. The Jews received Peter's explanation gladly, for we read: "When they heard this their doubts were silenced. They gave praise to God and said, 'This means that God has granted life-giving repentance to the Gentiles also' " (vs. 18, NEB).

Thus, it is perfectly clear that the middle wall of partition between faithful Jews and faithful Gentiles has been broken down completely; there is no part of it whatsoever that remains standing. Upon what basis then can anyone maintain that Israel "after the flesh" are a people of great privilege, to whom God gives blessings, care, and attention above anyone else?

A Surprising Element in Israel's Recovery

Some people argue that there are still a number of predictions concerning the Jewish people that have not yet been fulfilled. The prophets of old have spoken clearly about Israel's recovery, they remind us. God has promised to return to Israel and rebuild the fallen house of David. God has promised to reconstruct the city's ruins and set it up again. How should we understand these predictions? During the notable council of Acts 15, which took place in Jerusalem, the leading brethren discussed important questions and called attention to valuable information regarding the prophecies regarding Israel's recovery. What they said may surprise you as we use the lens of our discovery to review the records once again.

A difference of opinion arose in the early church concerning the rite of circumcision and other ceremonial *mitzvoth* in the law.[18] Those at odds agreed to consult the apostles and elders in a meeting at Jerusalem. Messianic believers from among the Pharisees urged, at the meeting, that the Gentiles must be circumcised and that they needed

---

18   As a result of the decision of this church council, the early "Christians and Jewish-Christian sects" (collectively known as the *minim*) "gave special importance to the Ten Commandments, which continued to be binding" "rather than the practical *mizvot*. "As a result of this, the rabbis cancelled the saying of the Ten Commandments together with the paragraphs of the *Shema* prayer, so that no-one should mistakenly think that the *mitzvot* included in the Ten Commandments were more binding than the rest of the *mitzot* in the *Torah*, as the *minim* claimed" (Aharon Oppenheimer, "Removing the Decalogue," *The Decalogue in Jewish and Christian Tradition* [New York: T&T Clark, 2011], Yair Hoffman and Henning Graf Reventlow, editors, p. 99).

Part 2 ISRAEL AND THE NEW TESTAMENT 65

to obey the law of Moses.[19] After much discussion, Peter stood up and rehearsed his experiences with the Gentile believers. He pointed out: "And God, who can read men's minds, showed his approval of them by giving the Holy Spirit to them, as he did to us. He made no difference between them and us; for he purified their hearts by faith. Then why do you now provoke God by laying on the shoulders of these converts a yoke which neither we nor our fathers were able to bear? No, we believe that it is by the grace of the Lord Jesus that we are saved, and so are they" (Acts 15:10, 11, NEB). The assembly listened quietly as Paul and Barnabas gave their wonderful account of the things that God had accomplished among the Gentiles. Luke rehearses what happened next:

> When they had finished speaking, James summed up: "My friends," he said, "listen to me, Simeon has told how it first happened that God took notice of the Gentiles, to choose from among them a people to bear his name; and this agrees with the words of the prophets, as Scripture has it: 'Therefore I will return and rebuild the fallen house of David; even from its ruins I will rebuild it, and set it up again, that they may seek the Lord—all the rest of mankind, and the Gentiles, whom I have claimed for my own. Thus says the Lord, whose work it is, made known long ago.'" (Acts 15:16–18, NEB).

James's conclusion is very important. It gives a sound biblical answer to a problem that concerns many people interested in Israel.

Consider what James pointed out. He referred to Simeon Peter's wonderful experience and to the miracles and wonders that God had wrought through Paul and Barnabas among the Gentiles as evidence that God had taken notice of the Gentiles, to choose from among them a people to bear His name—in agreement with the words of the prophets. James then quoted the very important prophecy of Amos: "Thereafter I will return and rebuild the fallen house of David; even from its

---

19　This was counter to the teaching of the Law itself, which only requires that Gentiles be circumcised if they wish to partake of the Passover feast (Exod. 12:48); otherwise, according to "[the Law of] Moses" which was "read in the synagogues every sabbath day" (Acts 15:21), the "strangers," or Gentiles, were only required to "abstain from pollutions of idols" (cf. Lev. 17:7, 8), "and *from* fornication" (cf. Lev. 18:24–26), "and *from* things strangled" (cf. Lev. 17:15), "and *from* blood" (cf. Lev. 17:10–12).

ruins I will rebuild it, and set it up again" (cf. Amos 9:11). What this is saying is that the fallen house of David was being rebuilt *through the believing Gentiles*. Amazingly, the words of the prophets about the promised restoration of Israel were in agreement with the wonderful things that God was doing for the Gentiles. They had received the Holy Spirit and were chosen by God to bear His name. Through faith they had now become a chosen generation, "a dedicated nation, and a people claimed by God for his own, to proclaim the triumphs of him who has called you out of darkness into his marvellous light. You are now the people of God, who once were not his people; outside his mercy once, you have now received his mercy" (1 Peter 2:9, 10, NEB). Just as Jesus said, God's kingdom has been taken away from the unrepentant Jews and given to a nation that yields fruit (Matt. 21:43).

The assembly at Jerusalem became fully convinced that the fallen house of David was to be rebuilt and set up again through believing Gentiles. They recognized that the words of the prophets of old supported this development and testified to it.

The assembly at Jerusalem became fully convinced that the fallen house of David was to be rebuilt and set up again through believing Gentiles.

Now, if we hold that the fallen house of David is to be rebuilt by Israel "after the flesh," how then do the words of the prophets fit in with Peter's declaration that God had visited the Gentiles and taken from them a people for His name? And how do the prophetic words of old fit in with Barnabas and Paul's rehearsal of the miraculous signs and wonders that God had performed among the Gentiles?

If the prophets of old only had in mind Israel "after the flesh" when they predicted the rebuilding of David's house, then the report of Peter, Barnabas and Paul about God's choosing of the Gentiles really does not relate to the prophecy James quoted regarding the building up of David's fallen house. What is more, it would say that the Scriptural basis for the decision of the assembly at Jerusalem was one big mistake. Is this right? No, it is impossible. Paul writes plainly that Scripture foresaw that God would justify believing Gentiles and bless them, as His people, through the blessing of Abraham. We read:

"Scripture foresaw that God would justify the Gentiles by faith, and announced the gospel in advance to Abraham: 'All nations will be blessed through you.' So those who rely on faith are blessed along with Abraham, the man of faith" (Gal. 3:8, 9, NIV).

Thus, we can confidently proclaim that the fallen house of David is rebuilt by faithful Gentiles who are no longer aliens, strangers or foreigners, but fellow-citizens of the household of God (cf. Eph. 2:12, 19).

David's fallen house is being rebuilt by the "other sheep" that Christ was to bring in as being part of a single fold (cf. John 10:16).

The believing Gentiles, who are grafted into the olive tree, thereby becoming part of it, are the ones through whom David's fallen house will be built and set up again (cf. Rom. 11:17; Acts 15:16).

Circumcised Inside

The assembly at Jerusalem came to the conclusion that the Gentile believers did not need to be circumcised (Acts 15:1, 20). Circumcision was a necessary ritual for Abraham's posterity. It was an outward sign of being set apart for God's service; it was a pledge for those receiving it that they would keep God's covenant, obey His law and remain separate from idolatry. Unfortunately, because of their unbelief, Israel as a nation did not generally live up to their pledge, and the rite of circumcision lost its significance for most people. Says the prophet: "I have spread out my hands all the day unto a rebellious people which walketh in a way *that was* not good, after their own thoughts ..." (Isa. 65:2). Through circumcision, believing strangers, or Gentiles, received admission into the commonwealth of Israel. However, since God calls all believers in one body, circumcision no longer segregates Jews and Gentiles. Thus, the apostle Paul writes: "Circumcision is nothing and uncircumcision is nothing, but the keeping of the commandments of God" (1 Cor. 7:19). Paul reasons that Abraham was also the father of the uncircumcised since his faith was counted to him as righteousness while he was yet uncircumcised (Rom. 4:9–11). Neither does circumcision make the Jews superior to other people. Paul asks the believing Romans: "Therefore, if an uncircumcised man keep the righteous requirements of the law, will not his uncircumcision be counted as circumcision?" (Rom. 2:26, NKJV). Obviously, faithfully obeying God's law does not require being circumcised. Paul then gives a definition of a true Jew: "For he is not a Jew, which is one outwardly; neither *is that* circumcision, which is outward in the flesh: But he *is* a Jew, which is one inwardly; and circumcision *is that* of the heart, in the spirit, *and* not in the letter; whose praise *is* not of men, but of God" (vss. 28, 29). He who is outwardly circumcised may be a Jew, but if he is not spiritually minded, then he is not at peace with God. In the same letter, Paul writes: "For to be carnally minded *is* death; but to be spiritually minded *is* life and peace.... So then they that are in the flesh cannot please God.... Now if any man have not the Spirit of Christ, he is none of his" (Rom. 8:6, 8, 9). Most definitely, it is the inward circumcision of the heart that matters. Being spiritually minded means having the Spirit of Christ and being guided daily by Him. Paul continues: "For as many as are led by the Spirit of God, they are the sons of God.... And if children, then heirs; heirs of God, and joint-heirs with Christ ..." (vss. 14, 17). Thus, Jewish children "after the flesh" are clearly without hope if they are not inwardly circumcised and have not accepted Christ. They are not the sons of God nor are they heirs unless they are spiritually minded and led by God's Spirit. The apostle explains: "Not as though the word of God hath taken none effect. For they *are* not all Israel, which are of Israel: Neither, because they are the seed of Abraham, *are they* all children: but, In Isaac shall thy seed be called. That is, They which are the children of the flesh, these *are* not the children of God: but the children of the promise are counted for the seed" (Rom. 9:6–8).

Paul quotes Old Testament prophecies that predict that many who are not God's people will be called sons of the living God, while only a remnant of the literal Jews will be saved (Rom. 9:25–29). Paul concludes: "Then what are we to say? That Gentiles, who made no effort after righteousness, nevertheless achieved it, a righteousness based on faith; whereas Israel made great efforts after a law of righteousness, but never attained to it. Why was this? Because their efforts were not based on faith, but (as they supposed) on deeds. They stumbled over the 'stumbling-stone' mentioned in Scripture: 'Here I lay in Zion a stumbling-stone and a rock to trip them up; but he who has faith in him will not be put to shame' " (Rom. 9:30–33, NEB).

Consequently, we must recognize that God's chosen people are not the children of the flesh. Rather, God's chosen people are the children of the promise, the children of faith. Paul gives the connection: "That the blessing of Abraham might come on the Gentiles through Jesus Christ; that we might receive the promise of the Spirit through faith ... that the promise by faith of Jesus Christ might be given to them that believe" (Gal. 3:14, 22).

Those who believe are the children of the promise; they are Abraham's seed. They are the true Israel, and it does not make any difference whether they are Jewish believers or Gentile believers, all are one in Christ Jesus. Israel is formed solely by children of the promise of the Spirit. Only when a descendant of Israel is led by God's Spirit and accepts Christ faithfully will he or she be a true Israelite. Nathanael was one of those true Israelites. When Jesus saw him coming, He said of him: "Behold an Israelite indeed, in whom is no guile!" (John 1:47). Nathanael was among the first to display his faith through his wonderful testimony about Jesus: "Rabbi, thou art the Son of God; thou art the King of Israel" (vs. 49). The Israel of which Paul is speaking is not a literal Israel "after the flesh," but it is an Israel bound and guided by the Spirit; a spiritual Israel made up of true Israelites. We should, therefore, keep in mind that, in Christ Jesus, spiritual Israel comes into focus while literal Israel fades away because of their unbelief.

Those who think that God will do great things for the Jews in Palestine need to be prepared for great disappointment, for only spiritual Israel matters.

Those who think that God will do great things for the Jews in Palestine need to be prepared for great disappointment, for only spiritual Israel matters.

The Olive Tree

The apostle Paul raises the question: "Hath God cast away his people?" Then he answers his own question: "God forbid. For I also am an Israelite, of the seed of Abraham, *of* the tribe of Benjamin" (Rom. 11:1). Paul calls attention to the faithful remnant, who are such by grace and not by works. He explains that the rest of Israel have been blinded and have stumbled and fallen that "through their fall salvation *is come* unto the Gentiles ..." (Rom. 11:11). Paul borrows from the picture of the olive tree in Jeremiah to illustrate the houses of Israel and Judah (Jer. 11:16, 17). In his adapted picture, the unfaithful branches of the olive tree are broken off and wild olive branches, representing Gentile believers of faith, are grafted in among the remaining faithful branches of Israel (Rom. 11:17, 20). Yet, there is still hope for the broken branches. If unfaithful Israelites turn from their unbelief, they "shall be graffed in: for God is able to graff them in again" (vs. 23). Through faith, Jewish and Gentile true Israelites share together, as one body, in the blessings of the same root and fatness of the one olive tree that is a picture of Israel. This confirms, once again, that faithful Jews together with faithful Gentiles are the true Israel of God.

Paul then writes: "For I would not, brethren, that ye should be ignorant of this mystery ... that blindness in part is happened to Israel, until the fulness of the Gentiles be come in" (vs. 25).

What are we to understand by the phrase, "this mystery"? The partial blindness of Israel, which caused their being broken off, has much to do with the coming in of the fullness of the Gentiles (Rom. 11:19, 20). In his letter to the Ephesians, Paul expanded upon the mystery of Christ revealed to him: "Which in other ages was not made known unto the sons of men, as it is now revealed unto his holy apostles and prophets by the Spirit; that the Gentiles should be fellowheirs and of the same body, and partakers of his promise in Christ by the gospel ..." (Eph. 3:4–6). Israel is not entirely blinded; there is a remaining, chosen and faithful remnant. Therefore, not all of the branches were broken off, just *some* of them (Rom. 11:17).

Now then, how does the fullness of the Gentiles come in? How are they made fellowheirs, fellowcitizens of the same body, of the household of God? How are they made partakers of the promise in Christ Jesus? Which picture has Paul used to illustrate the entrance of the Gentiles into true Israel? As we have noticed already, Paul explained that the Gentiles, being from the wild olive tree, have been grafted in among the faithful Jewish branches of Israel, thereby becoming partakers of the root and fatness of the noble olive tree. With this in mind, we will now consider the enigmatic phrase: "And so all Israel shall be saved ..." (vs. 26). Does this phrase legitimately support the millennial dream of the final conversion of all the Jews?

Part 2 ISRAEL AND THE NEW TESTAMENT 71

Very old olive trees in the Garden of Gethsemane

"All" of Which "Israel"?

What did Paul mean by "all Israel"? Did he mean literal Jews—Israel "after the flesh"? If he did, then the grafting in of the Gentiles would be an incomprehensible charade—to be grafted into the olive tree without belonging to it. How can they partake of the root and fatness of the olive and yet stand on the outside? What then is the purpose of being grafted? Are they grafted in to remain strangers? That would mean that there is still a great difference between Jews and Gentiles and that the partition wall has not been broken down. No, the mystery of Christ, revealed by the Spirit is that faithful Gentiles are no more strangers and foreigners but fellow-citizens of God's household and partakers of the promise. They belong fully to the Israel of God. And that is, without a doubt, precisely what Paul explained with the illustration of the grafting of the olive tree. He described the Gentiles as being grafted in among them *and with them* partaking of the root and fatness of the olive tree (Rom. 11:17). If the grafted Gentiles partake *with them*—that is, with the branches of Israel—of the blessings of the olive, then it is absolutely impossible that the Gentiles do not belong to Israel or that they remain separate from Israel on the outside. No, Paul declares that they are part of "the same body" (Eph. 3:6).

Earlier in Romans, Paul had stated: "For they are not all Israel, which are of Israel: Neither, because they are the seed of Abraham, are they all children: but, In Isaac shall thy seed be called. That is, They which are the children of the flesh, these are not the children of God: but the children of the promise are counted for the seed" (Rom. 9:6–8). Paul lays out a paradox, an apparent contradiction of terms: *not all* of Israel are *of Israel*. Two chapters later, he declares: "And so *all Israel* shall be saved." How can we understand Paul to mean that all Israel "after the flesh" will be saved? How can this possibly mean that every Jew will be saved? Are the chosen Gentile saints left standing outside because they are not literal Jews, because they are not part of the Israelites? Is such a view in harmony with what Paul revealed about the "mystery of Christ"?

Notwithstanding the clear Scripture passages that indicate that Jews and Gentiles are both equally and fully God's children through faith, many people fervently believe that Jewish Israel holds a special place with God above the Gentiles, that in some way they are God's "favorites." They take the statements in Romans 11 to mean that, when the fullness of the Gentiles has come in, all Jewish Israel will be saved. They believe that through God's doing all Jewish Israel will be then converted and accept their Deliverer, coming from Sion, who will "turn away ungodliness from Jacob" and "take away their sins" (Rom. 11:26, 27). Then they believe that Israel will be gloriously established and that Christ will be Israel's King on David's throne in Jerusalem.

It should be noted, however, that Paul does not say: *Then* all Israel shall be saved, as if he were referring to a certain moment in time when the fullness of the Gentiles would have come in and *then* all Israel would be saved. No, the idea of time is not part of Paul's statement. He clearly says: "*And so* all Israel shall be saved." This wording is a conclusion about "all Israel" being saved *in the way he just has explained*. That is, faithful Jews together with faithful Gentiles, who were grafted in among them, are the "*all Israel"* who will be saved. The phrase "until the fullness of the Gentiles be come in" points to their opportunity not being cut short for becoming faithful. Thus, all those who will answer God's call shall have entered in; they are all counted; their fullness will come in; not one will be lacking. Until that moment is reached, there will still be compassionate grace for everyone, including Jews who choose to abandon unbelief. And, thus, all Israel—that is, *all Jews and Gentiles who answer God's call*—will be saved.

Faithful Jews together with faithful Gentiles, who were grafted in among them, are the "all Israel" who will be saved.

Some may quote Paul's words to prove their millennial dream of a whole Jewish conversion: "And so all Israel shall be saved: as it is written, There shall come out of Sion the Deliverer, and shall turn away ungodliness from Jacob: For this *is* my covenant unto them, when I shall take away their sins" (Rom. 11:26, 27). They may ask: Does this not clearly indicate that the ungodliness and sins of all Israel will be done away by the coming Deliverer from Sion?

Yet, let us have a closer look at these inspired words. Paul refers to the words of the prophet Isaiah: "And the Redeemer shall come to Zion, and unto them that turn from transgression in Jacob, saith the LORD" (Isa. 59:20). Did Isaiah and Paul really believe that, with the coming of the Deliverer, or Redeemer, all Jewish Israel will be cleansed and be saved? Notice that Paul also quoted Isaiah a little earlier: "Esaias also crieth concerning Israel, Though the number of the children of Israel be as the sand of the sea, a remnant shall be saved" (Rom. 9:27; cf. Isa. 10:22). Thus, Paul and Isaiah believed that only a remnant of Jewish Israel will be saved. And if we read the words of Isaiah to which Paul referred in chapter 11, it is clear that the Deliverer will only come to those "that turn from transgression in Jacob ..." Will all of Israel turn from transgression? No, the prophet has pointed out that only a remnant will be faithful. It is to these that the Deliverer comes to take away their sins. The *New International Version* says: " 'The Redeemer will come to Zion, to those in Jacob who repent of their sins,' declares the LORD" (Isa. 59:20). Thus, it is clear that the Redeemer comes to the repentant—and not the unfaithful—Israelites. Moreover, Paul has explained what happened to the unrepentant branches. They were broken off, while believing Gentiles were grafted in to share together with the true Israelite branches the blessings of the olive tree.

Paul's desire and prayer to God for the Israelites is "that they might be saved" (Rom. 10:1), but he did not expect that *all* of Jewish Israel would be saved. He wrote: "If by any means I may provoke to emulation *them which are* my flesh, and might save some of them" (Rom. 11:14). Paul, in his days, hoped that *some* of his fellow Jews might be saved, and he did not in any way indicate that in the future *all* Jews will somehow become faithful and be saved.

If Paul really did mean that all Israel "after the flesh" would be saved, and his message were in harmony with the prophets, why then did he not quote some of the prophetic passages, which many today are so convinced refer to Israel's bright recovery in the last days? If so clearly prophesied, it would have been easy for Paul to have quoted them, but he did not. He knew better!

Paul's Continual Sorrow

Paul also testified: "... I have great heaviness and continual sorrow in my heart. For I could wish that myself were accursed from Christ for my brethren, my kinsmen according to the flesh: Who are Israelites ..." (Rom. 9:2–4). Now if Paul intended to make clear that all Israelites—that is, every Jew—would be saved, why then was he so gloomy, having great heaviness and continual sorrow in his heart? If all Israelites would be saved would that not have been a great comfort to the apostle?

Many believe that the graves will be opened and the houses of Judah and Israel will arise and be united in a mighty and prosperous kingdom. If that were true, why was Paul not in a better mood? Is it not puzzling that Israel's bright future did not for even one moment lift up his gloomy feelings? But, no, he said, the sorrow in his heart was *continual*, without a moment of relief. Why was that so? Simply because the apostle knew the reality of the situation and did not expect a glorious future for the literal Jews at the end of time.

Others who refer to a glorious future for literal Israel refer to Paul's words, "For the gifts and calling of God *are* without repentance. For as ye [Gentiles] in times past have not believed God, yet have now obtained mercy through their unbelief: Even so have these also now not believed, that through your mercy they also may obtain mercy. For God hath concluded them all in unbelief, that he might have mercy upon all" (Rom. 11:29–32).

Therefore, some people conclude, on the basis of this passage, that unbelieving Israel will once again obtain mercy and be restored at the end of time. Note well, however, what the text actually says. It says: "… that through your mercy they also *may* obtain mercy." It does not say that they *will* obtain mercy. No, it says that they *can* obtain mercy *if* they do not remain in their unbelief, for then they will be grafted back in. That is what Paul explained a few verses earlier (vs. 23). God subjected them all to unbelief that He might have mercy upon all—both Jews and Gentiles alike—when they come to repentance.

Do any of these texts mention a merciful restoration of the Jewish Israelites in the future? Is there any indication that the Jews had to wait until the end of time to receive mercy? It is interesting to note that several Bible manuscripts for verse 31—although not all—have the word "*now*" two times, causing the phrase to read: "so they too have *now* become disobedient in order that they too may *now* receive mercy as a result of God's mercy to you" (NIV, emphasis added); "so they have *now* been disobedient so that through the mercy you are enjoying they may *now* receive mercy" (Berkeley, emphasis added); "even so have these also *now* been disobedient, that by the mercy shown to you they also may *now* obtain mercy" (ASV, emphasis added).

Thus, God's mercy for Israelites who turn to Him in faithfulness is not something in the far distant future; it is instantaneous.

> *God's mercy for Israelites who turn to Him in faithfulness is not something in the far distant future; it is instantaneous.*

The thought that Paul presented is that the purpose for the provoking of unbelieving Jews to jealousy when they see the believing Gentiles as objects of God's mercy was to cause some to repent, receive God's mercy and be saved (Rom. 10:19; 11:11, 14).

The Meaning of the "Gentile Fullness"

Paul wrote that a partial blindness "is happened to Israel, until the fulness of the Gentiles be come in" (Rom. 11:25). This means, he says, that, through the blindness and fall of Israel, salvation has come to the Gentiles, that their transgression means riches for the world, and their casting away is the reconciliation of the world (Rom. 11:11, 12, 15). This startling fall of Israel has opened, as it were, a door for the Gentiles. Yet, how will we know when the full number of the Gentiles have entered in?

When will the entire number of the called and chosen saints of the Gentile world have joined the Israel of God? The answer is not difficult: It will be at the end of the world when the preaching of the gospel is finished. Until that moment, the ministry of grace of the gospel of Jesus Christ is still valid. Until that moment, the door is open to all repentant sinners, including repentant Jews. Jesus said: "And this gospel of the kingdom shall be preached in all the world for a witness unto all nations; and then shall the end come" (Matt. 24:14). While the gospel call continues and the end has not yet come, every repentant sinner of all nations—whether Jew or Gentile, it makes no difference—can still turn to the Lord, join the Israel of God and be saved.

It must be emphasized that only those who walk according to the rule of a new creation are true Israelites. Paul explains: "Neither circumcision nor uncircumcision means anything; what counts is the new creation. Peace and mercy to all who follow this rule—to the Israel of God" (Gal. 6:15, 16, NIV). The Berkeley Version says: "For neither circumcision nor the lack of it is important, but a new creation counts, and those who behave by this rule, peace and mercy be upon them, even on the Israel of God."

Part 2 ISRAEL AND THE NEW TESTAMENT

Thus, it is clear that the Israel of God is made up of believers who are a new creation. Only those who are born again of the Spirit can enter the kingdom of God and be saved (2 Cor. 5:17; Eph. 2:10; 4:24; John 3:3, 5, 6).

Kenneth S. Wuest's comment aptly explains: "Those therefore, who order their lives by the Holy Spirit's control, constitute the true Israel of God, not the Jews who have the name of Israel but are only children of Abraham after the flesh. The Greek word for 'and' also has the meaning of 'even' in some contexts. We translate here, 'even the Israel of God' as identifying those who 'walk according to this rule.' "[20]

When the apostle has previously declared, "For they are not all Israel, which are of Israel," his use of the words "all Israel" and "Israel of God" cannot be construed to include all Jews or Israelites "after the flesh." No, there is enough evidence that he includes in these terms only true and faithful Israelites, both of Jewish and Gentile stock. That Paul did not expect a conversion of all Israel "after the flesh" is also indicated in his words elsewhere about the Jews: "Who both killed the Lord Jesus, and their own prophets, and have persecuted us; and they please not God, and are contrary to all men: Forbidding us to speak to the Gentiles that they might be saved, to fill up their sins alway: for the wrath is come upon them to the uttermost" (1 Thess. 2:15, 16). James Moffatt's translation says: "So they would fill up the measure of their sins to the last drop! But the Wrath is on them to the bitter end!"

On the phrase, "wrath is come upon them to the uttermost," Anglican Bible scholar John Trapp commented: "Or, until the end: wrath is come upon them finally (*eis télos*), so as it shall never be removed ..."[21] We should understand this to exclude the faithful remnant among them.

Paul's statement is not in harmony with a bright recovery of the Jewish nation. Rather, it testifies that he did not believe in a future restoration of all Israel.

In the book of Hebrews is a summary, taken from the Psalms, of Israel's unbelief: "So, as the Holy Spirit says: 'Today, if you hear his voice, do not harden your hearts as you did in the rebellion, during the time of testing in the desert, where your fathers tested and tried me and for forty years saw what I did. That is why I was angry with that

---

20   Kenneth S. Wuest, *Galatians in the Greek New Testament for the English Reader* (Grand Rapids, MI: Eerdmans Publishing Co., 1944), p. 179.

21   John Trapp, *A Commentary on the Old and New Testaments* (Eureka, CA: Tanski Publishing, 1997), vol. 5, p. 625.

generation, and I said, "Their hearts are always going astray, and they have not known my ways." So I declared on oath in my anger, "They shall never enter my rest" ' " (Heb. 3:7–11, NIV; Ps. 95:8–11, NIV). There is in this statement an elliptic form of an oath, which God swore—an oath with a strong negative meaning—Never will they enter! It is very true that a large part of Israel did not enter the rest of the Promised Land but died in the wilderness. Yet, since the rest in Hebrews 3 and 4 prefigures the rest in the heavenly Canaan, there is still an urgent message of warning in this passage. Only obedient believers will enter into God's rest, but Israel "after the flesh" will never enter, and there is no indication whatsoever that the Jewish nation as a whole will be converted—only a remnant shall be saved. The apostle hoped that *some* might be provoked to jealousy and become faithful. Paul did not in any way picture a massive conversion of Jewish Israel somewhere in the future.

A Blessed Period of Restoration for the Jews?

If it were true that a blessed period of restoration is coming for the Jewish nation in which all Israel will be converted and saved, then it would certainly be desirable, if you are a Jew, to be alive during that time! Just think what it would mean to be born just in time to experience the conversion of all Israel and share in its bright revival! What a great privilege to be living during the most wonderful time of grace and mercy! But think of the unfortunate one who happened to be born a little too early. Talk about a birthright!

If God really is going to resurrect Judah and Israel from their graves to form a mighty kingdom on earth, as many people believe, why does He wait so long for Gentiles to come in before displaying His kindness and benevolence toward the Jews? Is it that God is insisting that they take turns—now, while it is the Gentiles' turn, the Jews have to wait until it is their turn before they come to God? Why does God not take away their blindness earlier? Why does He not bring about their conversion sooner? Why do they have to wait so long? Is God responsible for the Jews' blindness and unbelief? If He is, then why did Jesus weep over Jerusalem and lament: "... and all because you would not understand the time when God was visiting you" (Luke 19:44, Moffatt)?

*East Jerusalem, Russian Orthodox Church of Mary Magdalene
near the Garden of Gethsemane*

Even before the apostle Paul, Jesus had great heaviness and sorrow over Jerusalem's children. He would have liked very much for Israel to have recognized that which belonged to their peace. Jesus had, in spite of their rebellion and unbelief, great sympathy for Israel. He stood always ready to save them. He testified: "... how often would I have gathered thy children together, even as a hen gathereth her chickens under *her* wings, and ye would not!" (Matt. 23:37). Jesus would have delighted in taking Israel's blindness away and given them grace, peace and salvation. Yet, they did not want it. The problem was not with Christ or with God but with the unwillingness of Israel.

The apostle Paul refers to a prophecy of Isaiah in which God says to Israel: "... All day long I have stretched forth my hands unto a disobedient and gainsaying people" (Rom. 10:21; cf. Isa 65:2).

God is willing all day long. His compassionate grace for Israel does not belong merely to the future. Paul assures his readers that believing Gentiles "now have received mercy" and then he says of the Jews: "... so that to them too there may now be mercy" (Rom. 11:31, Weymouth).

No one needs to wait his turn. God will *always* be gracious to all who call upon His name. He "is rich unto all that call upon him" (Rom. 10:12). There is no shadow of partiality or discrimination with God. "For the eyes of the LORD run to and fro throughout the whole earth, to shew himself strong in the behalf of *them* whose heart *is* perfect toward him" (2 Chron. 16:9).

God is not one moment rich toward the Gentiles and then another moment rich toward the Jews. No, at all times He is rich toward all who call upon His name in faith. His eyes range through the whole earth to bring aid to all who trust in Him. The apostle Peter testified: "Of a truth I perceive that God is no respecter of persons: But in every nation he that feareth him, and worketh righteousness, is accepted with him" (Acts 10:34, 35). The *New International Version* says: "I now realize how true it is that God does not show favoritism but accepts from every nation the one who fears him and does what is right."

God has done everything to save Israel. He has stretched out His hands to them—"the whole day long"! And this He does to everyone of all nations. He is Lord of all and rich in blessing to all who call upon Him—without difference between Jew and Gentile (Rom. 10:12). Unfortunately, Israel was unwilling to respond in faith. God is at all times gracious and helpful. Yet, to receive His blessings and to be saved, one must be willing, show faith and be obedient. Israel's partial blindness did not remain because the time of their mercy had not yet come or because the fullness of the Gentiles had not gone in. No, Israel's partial blindness could not be taken away because Israel was disobedient and unfaithful and did not choose otherwise. It is because God foresaw that Israel's impenitence as a nation would remain until the end that the Bible declares: "… that blindness in part is happened to Israel, until the fulness of the Gentiles be come in" (Rom. 11:25). By the time the fulness has come in, it will be the end of time. However, every Israelite who calls upon the name of the Lord, abandoning unbelief, will be grafted back into the olive tree and be saved. That is what the apostle makes clear. Israel as a nation will never be converted, even though many individual Jews will turn to God in faithfulness and be saved. The prophets of old have prophesied it: Only a remnant will be saved!

The "Second Chance" is Today

The apostle Paul emphasized: "As God's fellow-workers we urge you not to receive God's grace in vain. For he says, 'In the time of my favor I heard you, and in the day of salvation I helped you.' I tell you, now is the time of God's favor, now is the day of salvation" (2 Cor. 6:1, 2, NIV). And in his letter, addressed to the Hebrews, he contrasted the "day of rebellion" with the day in the appeal in the Psalms: "To day if ye will hear his voice, harden not your hearts" (Heb. 4:7; cf. Psa. 95:7, 8). After the gospel of the kingdom has been preached in all the world and *the end has come* (Matt. 24:14), is it still possible that a special period of grace will be extended to Israel as a nation?

Many believe that Christ will descend upon the Mount of Olives and from there recover and rebuild the Jewish nation. They believe that the Jews will accept Jesus and be converted and then go out among the Gentiles as God's missionaries. They also believe that the city of Jerusalem will at that time become the center of worship for all nations (Isa. 56), that the temple will be rebuilt, that sacrifices will be brought, and that the Jewish festivals will be observed as all nations go up to Jerusalem for worship (Isa. 66). Though many are convinced of this scenario, is it true that there will be a second period of salvation on this earth after the preaching of the gospel has ceased and God's children have been taken to heaven? When the Word of God says: "… behold, now *is* the accepted time; behold, now *is* the day of salvation" (2 Cor. 6:2), is it possible that another time of acceptance will come around, giving another day of salvation? And when the Hebrews were exhorted: "To day if ye will hear his voice, harden not your hearts" (Heb. 4:7), should we postulate still another opportunity for them, so that, if they do not want to hear His voice now, they can respond to it the next time it comes? That would not be bad if it were possible, and it would certainly suit many people. If a Jew misses the boat now, no problem, he can catch the next. The thought of a second chance is certainly attractive, for it promises that all Jews will be converted, all will be prosperity and millennial peace, conversions will occur on a national and worldwide scale. The present preaching of the gospel pales in comparison with what is projected to happen during the millennial period with the other, second day of salvation. What a bright future! It is hard to believe that the apostle Paul carried such great heaviness and continual sorrow of heart (Rom. 9:2) with such a blessed future supposedly ahead for literal Israel. Or was Paul right in stressing that everyone must choose *now* because the day of salvation is *now*? There is no room in any of Paul's statements for a second chance after the return of Christ.

> *There is no room in any of Paul's statements for a second chance after the return of Christ.*

Paul says: "For I am not ashamed of the gospel of Christ: for it is the power of God unto salvation to every one that believeth; to the Jew first, and also to the Greek" (Rom. 1:16). Will God come up with another "power of God unto salvation" that reinstates sacrifices and the Jewish festivals? Is it conceivable that God's plan of salvation will return to the shadows and symbols that have already been fulfilled in Christ?

The apostle Paul wrote: "And now, my brothers, I must remind you of the gospel that I preached to you; the gospel which you received, on which you have taken your stand, and which is now bringing you salvation. Do you still hold fast the Gospel as I preached it to you? If not, your conversion was in vain" (1 Cor. 15:1, 2, NEB).

How very important it is to hold fast the gospel as it was preached by Paul! It is the only gospel that brings salvation. If we do not hold fast as to that which Paul preached, we have no hope, and our conversion is in vain. There is only one gospel to be preached in the whole world: "Go ye into all the world, and preach the gospel to every creature. He that believeth and is baptized shall be saved; but he that believeth not shall be damned" (Mark 16:15, 16). Does this one gospel leave room for a second opportunity to be saved? The text plainly says: "... but he that believeth not shall be damned." Could this really mean that he will be damned for the moment but then saved during the millennium? Notice that Christ does not come back to the earth to offer a second chance, but to punish the unbelievers: "He will punish those who do not know God and do not obey the gospel of our Lord Jesus. They will be punished with everlasting destruction ..." (2 Thess. 1:8, 9, NIV). The gospel of our Lord Jesus Christ is the only gospel by which we can be saved. The apostle Paul is very clear: "As we said before, so say I now again, If any *man* preach any other gospel unto you than that ye have received, let him be accursed" (Gal. 1:9). Thus, it is perfectly clear that there is only one gospel. The apostle emphasizes this very strongly: "But though we, or an angel from heaven, preach any other gospel unto you than that which we have preached unto you, let him be accursed" (Gal. 1:8). So we can be sure that there is no other gospel, and, therefore, it is absolutely impossible for there to be another gospel during the millennium with sacrifices and festivals, which were all fulfilled and brought to an end in Christ Jesus. According to Paul, those who preach another gospel are accursed!

Too Late Once the Door is Shut

The Bible makes plain that there is only one way of salvation and that everyone must choose now, for *now* is the day of salvation. It will soon be too late, and this warning applies also to the Jewish nation.

As Jesus was traveling to Jerusalem, someone asked Him if only a few would be saved. Jesus answered that many will seek to enter in and shall not be able. Jesus told His Jewish audience:

> When once the master of the house has got up and locked the door, you may stand outside and knock, and say, "Sir, let us in!", but he will only answer, "I do not know where you come from." Then you will begin to say, "we sat at table with you and you taught in our streets." But he will repeat, "I tell you, I do not know where you come from. Out of my sight, all of you, you and your wicked ways!" There will be wailing and grinding of teeth there, when you see Abraham,

Isaac, and Jacob, and all the prophets, in the kingdom of God, and yourselves thrown out. (Luke 13:25–28, NEB)

Do these words in any way indicate that there will be a second chance for a massive conversion? No, not at all. Once the door has been shut, it will not be opened again. They may plead to come in, but, no, they will only know the street. No Deliverer will come and remove wickedness from Jacob or take away their sins. No, that time is past; the day of salvation has gone by, and the answer is: *Depart from me, all you evildoers.* It will be as in the days of Noah. Once the door of the ark was shut, it would not be opened. Those who are faithful will be saved, while all the unbelievers will not get a new, second chance; they will be destroyed. In discussing the coming of Christ, the apostle Peter also compared it to the days of Noah. As the world perished through water, he says, so the earth is now kept in store for the fire of the Day of Judgment when all the ungodly will be destroyed. Peter also adds that scoffers will come in the last days, doubting the promise of the coming of Christ since all things continue as always. Peter then says: "The Lord is not slack concerning his promise, as some men count slackness; but is longsuffering to us-ward, not willing that any should perish, but that all should come to repentance" (2 Peter 3:9).

If the coming of Christ will be followed by a new period of grace in which people will be converted on a large scale, how are we then to understand Peter's words? If this were the case, would it not be desirable that this mad and sinful world should come to a quick end? Why would God need to demonstrate His patience in not being "willing that any should perish" (2 Peter 3:9) if a blessed period is ahead with massive conversions? If the popular view of a Jewish millennium of prosperity, peace and salvation for all were indeed biblically true, why would the Lord hold off His return so that all should come to repentance? Should not such a blessed period of repentance ahead be a good reason to have Christ's coming as soon as possible? Why then does He patiently wait? Would it not be that the faster this world of trouble and misery came to its end the better it would be? But, no, Scripture teaches: *Now* is the day of salvation; *now* only is it still possible to come to repentance. It will soon be too late. *Now* is your "second chance." Peter urges us, therefore, to live holy and godly lives, to make every effort to be found spotless, blameless and at peace with God. And Peter adds: "Bear in mind that our Lord's patience with us

Part 2 ISRAEL AND THE NEW TESTAMENT

is our salvation" (vs. 15, NEB). Peter clearly pictures our salvation *before* the coming of our Lord and not afterwards.

What a great disappointment the coming of Christ will be for those who have expected a period of grace when they find the door of salvation is actually closed. Jesus taught this truth in the parable of the five wise and five foolish virgins. While the foolish virgins went away to buy oil for their lamps, which they had forgotten to purchase before, the bridegroom came, "and they that were ready went in with him to the marriage: and the door was shut. Afterward came also the other virgins, saying, Lord, Lord, open to us. But he answered and said, Verily I say unto you, I know you not. Watch therefore, for ye know neither the day nor the hour wherein the Son of man cometh" (Matt. 25:10–13). Once again we see that there is no second chance for entering. The door was shut and not opened again. *Now* is the time to be ready. When Christ has come it will be too late.

The apostle Paul, speaking about Israel's failure to enter God's rest, in a letter specifically addressed to the Hebrews, quotes the words of David: "Again, he limiteth a certain day, saying in David, To day, after so long a time; as it is said, To day if ye will hear his voice, harden not your hearts" (Heb. 4:7; cf. Ps. 95:7, 8). Paul quotes David's words three times, apparently to emphasize the importance of answering God's voice *now* and not hardening one's heart (Heb. 3:7, 15; 4:7). Since many of the people of Israel did not enter the promised rest because of their unbelief, Paul uses this failure to excite the Hebrews, as well as the Gentiles, not to be unwilling but to make good use of the *present* day of salvation, wherein mercy is still offered. Again, this is not a day of mercy offered in the distant future, no, it is *today*; it is *now*, and there is no indication anywhere that God will once more set another day of opportunity. Our "second chance" is every "today" that God has given us.

Paul did not believe that the Jewish nation was still God's elect. He had made plain that believing Gentiles have taken their place as fellow-citizens of God's household and that they are now God's chosen people.

Paul did not believe that the Jewish nation was still God's elect. He had made plain that believing Gentiles have taken their place as fellow-citizens of God's household and that they are now God's chosen people. *Harper's Bible Dictionary* declares: "To Paul God's chosen people were not Israel—who had rejected the Gospel in spite of having received the Law and the Messiah—but Christians. To him the 'elect' and the 'saints' were Abraham's spiritual but not physical descendants (Rom. 2:28f., 4:9ff.). The New Testament supplanted Israel with the church. Israel had failed, but not God (Rom. 9–11)."[22]

An Obsolete Ceremonial System Revived?

The Bible teaches us that all those who are disobedient to the gospel of our Lord Jesus Christ, will "be punished with everlasting destruction from the presence of the Lord, and from the glory of his power; When he shall come to be glorified in his saints, and to be admired in all them that believe ..." (2 Thess. 1:9, 10).

However, according to the teachings of many, Israel as a whole will be converted and blessed with all that which the fleshly heart desires: prosperity, safety, peace, and national greatness. There will be no war, no ferocious animals, and the earth will yield its fullness.

The temple at Jerusalem will be rebuilt, and the Jews will evangelize among the nations then living on the earth, and they will all go up to Jerusalem to worship. But the worship of Jerusalem will only be a formal, legal system of ceremonies, symbols and sacrifices, just as ancient Israel used to practice, and the Old Testament feasts will also be celebrated. The services that were done away by Christ's sacrifice, when He was offered "once and for all," will be once again revived, they say (Heb. 10:10). Yet, going back to the shadows and symbols fulfilled in Christ is a clear rejection of the reality of His finished, redeeming work. It signifies that Christ's sacrifice has had no effect. How could it ever be pleasing and acceptable to God to offer animal sacrifices again when the Lamb of God was slain as a perfect and sufficient sacrifice to save everyone who accepts Him and calls upon His name?

---

22   Madelaine S. Miller, J. Lane Miller, *Harper's Bible Dictionary* (New York: Harper & Row, 1952), p. 293. Some believe that this gives the church authority to change God's laws, but such a change is only described in Scripture as an act against the God and His people (Dan. 7:25). To the contrary, the "New Covenant," which is between God and Israel, is concerning submitting to having God's laws written in the heart and mind (Heb. 8:10; 10:16). It does not give the church authority to change God's laws.

Paul wrote to the Hebrews about Christ: " 'Sacrifices and offerings, whole-offerings and sin-offerings, thou didst not desire nor delight in'—although the Law prescribes them—and then he says, 'I have come to do thy will.' He thus *annuls the former* to establish the latter. And it is by the will of God that we have been consecrated, through the offering of the body of Jesus Christ once and for all" (Heb. 10:8–10, NEB, emphasis added).

Thus, it is clear that the former law of sacrifices is annulled, while the latter, the offering of the body of Jesus, once for all, is established as the true means of our consecration. Animal blood could not take away sins (vs. 4), and God did not delight in the sacrifices prescribed by the law. Redemption came through Jesus—the perfect human substitute of infinite merit offered for humankind. In submission to God's will, Christ took upon Him this redemptive role and offered His body a ransom for all people.

But the teaching of dispensationalism is that those who are living on the earth after Christ returns have not been sanctified through the offering of the body of Christ. Rejecting the gospel call, they were not taken up in glory into God's kingdom. At Christ's coming they were not in a moment, in the twinkling of an eye, at the last trump, changed into immortality (1 Cor. 15:52, 53). They are no part of God's spiritual kingdom of heaven. They remain on this earth to be part of an earthly kingdom. But this human view of things is completely out of harmony with God's everlasting Word of truth.

The Bible clearly teaches that there is salvation only in God's heavenly kingdom. Outside is only destruction. Jesus taught this very clearly in several parables. "The kingdom of heaven," He declared, "is likened unto a man which sowed good seed in his field ..." (Matt. 13:24). The wheat he gathered into the barn, while the tares he had bound in bundles to be burned (vss. 30, 40). At the harvest, Jesus said, the angels shall gather out "all things that offend, and them which do iniquity; and shall cast them into a furnace of fire" (vss. 41, 42). But the righteous shall "shine forth as the sun in the kingdom of their Father" (vs. 43).

And again, Jesus declared, "the kingdom of heaven is like unto a net, that was cast into the sea, and gathered of every kind: which, when it was full, they drew to shore, and sat down, and gathered the good into vessels, but cast the bad away" (Matt. 13:47, 48). Does the parable make provision for the bad to be gathered into some other vessel? Will the good be gathered into God's kingdom of heaven and the bad into an earthly kingdom under a second chance? Not in the least.

Notice how Jesus finishes the parable: "So shall it be at the end of the world: the angels shall come forth, and sever the wicked from among the just, and shall cast them into the furnace of fire ..." (vss. 49, 50). Jesus clearly taught that there are only two groups, those who do the will of God and enter the kingdom of heaven and those who work iniquity, whom He declares He does not know, and are sent away. Hear Jesus' solemn sentence: "I never knew you: depart from me, ye that work iniquity" (Matt. 7:23).

Jesus' Two Ways ... Plus One?

Jesus declared that there is only one way to life. The wide gate and the broad road lead to destruction, "but the gate that leads to life is small and the road is narrow ..." (Matt. 7:14, NEB). Despite the clarity of Jesus' statement, is it possible that there is, aside from these two roads, yet another, alternate gate that allows passage to a road that is neither wide nor narrow, but of a size in between? If the narrow road leads to life in God's *heavenly* kingdom and the broad road to perdition, could this in-between road lead to an *earthly* kingdom? Although many believe in a third possibility, the Bible provides no basis whatsoever for such an alternate road. Nowhere in the Bible is there any indication that there are two ways that lead to life—one to *heavenly* life and one to *earthly* life. No, all who will be saved, will be *one* flock, and they will not make up two separate groups. If the faithful church is glorified in God's heavenly kingdom while those "left behind" find life in an earthly kingdom, then there is not one flock but two—a heavenly and an earthly. This would mean that there would also be two sheepfolds, each with its own door—in direct contradiction of Jesus' pronouncement. Conceiving of a second way of life is completely against the teaching of the Bible. It is human fantasy. There is only one way that leads to life, and there shall be only one flock, one fold, one door and one shepherd (John 10:1–16).

When Christ comes to gather His saints into His kingdom, will there then be people alive, "left behind," on this earth? From Jesus' comparison of His coming with the days of Noah and of Lot, it is certain that there will be no people "left behind" on planet Earth. Except Noah and his family, no one was saved. The flood destroyed them all. And so it was in the days of Lot. When Lot and his family left Sodom, it rained fire and brimstone, and destroyed everyone left behind (Luke 17:26–30).

The prophets of old prophesied that the earth will be made desolate and all sinners will be destroyed: "Behold, the day of the Lord cometh, cruel both with wrath and fierce anger, to lay the land desolate: and he shall destroy the sinners thereof out of it" (Isa. 13:9). On that day the trumpet will sound; there will be an earthquake and the land will be made desolate, without any people left alive: Jeremiah describes the desolation: "How long must I see the battle standard and hear the sound of the trumpet? ... I looked at the earth, and it was formless and empty; and at the heavens, and their light was gone. I looked at the mountains, and they were quaking; all the hills were swaying. I looked, and there were no people; every bird in the sky had flown away. I looked, and the fruitful land was a desert; all its towns lay in ruins before the Lord, before his fierce anger" (Jer. 4:21, 23–26, NIV).

Zephaniah describes the earth being completely emptied of all living things, with no humans or animals left alive: " 'I will completely remove all things from the face of the earth,' declares the Lord. 'I will remove man and beast; I will remove the birds of the sky and the fish of the sea, and the ruins along with the wicked; and I will cut off man from the face of the earth,' declares the Lord" (Zeph. 1:2, 3, NASB). Zephaniah continues by describing the punishment of those invited to the Lord God's sacrifice who are clothed in strange apparel: "Be silent before the Lord God! For the day of the Lord is near, for the Lord has prepared a sacrifice, He has consecrated His guests. Then it will come about on the day of the Lord's sacrifice, that I will punish the princes, the king's sons, and all who clothe themselves with foreign garments" (vss. 7, 8, NASB). Similarly, Jesus taught, in the parable of the wedding banquet, that the guest without a wedding garment was thrown outside into the darkness (Matt. 22:11–13).

Zephaniah also describes the destruction of sinners and the uninhabited earth: "And I will bring distress on men so that they will walk like the blind, because they have sinned against the Lord; and their blood will be poured out like dust and their flesh like dung. Neither their silver nor their gold will be able to deliver them on the day of the Lord's wrath; and all the earth will be devoured in the fire of His jealousy, for He will make *a complete end*, indeed a terrifying one, of all the inhabitants of the earth" (Zeph. 1:17, 18, NASB, emphasis added).

These prophets of old addressed their messages to the children of Israel, so we can be sure that the children of Israel had no bright prospect of a millennial recovery as a nation. In various places, the Bible undeniably teaches that, on the day of the Lord, which is Christ's return, He will take His children home into His Father's house. They are the blessed faithful who are called to the marriage supper of the Lamb (Rev. 19:9). In these same passages, the Bible also teaches that all the unfaithful will be punished, that they will be destroyed, and the earth will be left without inhabitants.

When Christ comes, the nations will be gathered before Him "and he shall separate them one from another, as a shepherd divideth his sheep from the goats: And he shall set the sheep on his right hand, but the goats on the left. Then shall the King say unto them on his right hand, Come, ye blessed of my Father, inherit the kingdom prepared for you from the foundation of the world: ... Then shall he say also unto them on the left hand, Depart from me, ye cursed, into everlasting fire ..." (Matt. 25:32–34, 41). Once again, we hear Jesus pointing to just two groups—on the right hand are the blessed ones who inherit God's kingdom and on the left hand are the cursed ones who are destroyed. There is no hint whatsoever of a third group of saved people in an earthly, millennial kingdom.

There is no hint whatsoever of a third group of saved people in an earthly, millennial kingdom.

The Times of the Gentiles

Jesus warned that Jerusalem would be devastated: "... there shall be great distress in the land, and wrath upon this people. And they shall fall by the edge of the sword, and shall be led away captive into all nations: and Jerusalem shall be trodden down of the Gentiles, until the times of the Gentiles be fulfilled" (Luke 21:23, 24).

He said that Jerusalem will be trodden down of the Gentiles until their times be fulfilled. When will their times be fulfilled, and what will happen then? Many people repeat the belief that Israel will be blessed and restored as God's chosen nation and Jerusalem will be a prosperous city where the Messiah will sit on David's throne and reign over the world.

The great question is, however: Is there any indication that that was in Christ's mind or that it was His intention that any come to that belief? Jesus said nothing about Israel's recovery as His chosen nation. He only said that Jerusalem will be trodden down of the Gentiles until their times be fulfilled. That is all that He said. So shall it be—Jerusalem will be a city, trampled down. Jesus did not explain what will happen when the times of the Gentiles are fulfilled. He did not say anything about that. It is remarkable then that, where Jesus kept silence, many people think they know precisely what will happen.

Is there any reason to believe that Jerusalem will soon be no longer trodden down by the Gentiles? Jesus spoke about Jerusalem only in a negative sense—Jerusalem, which killed the prophets and stoned those sent to her. Jesus pronounced that ominous sentence: "*Your* house is left *unto you* desolate" (Matt. 23:37, 38), and He spoke about destruction, vengeance, distress and wrath (Luke 21:20–23). Moreover, Paul declared: "But [God's] wrath has come upon them at last [completely and forever]" (1 Thess. 2:16, AMP). So there is no reason to believe that God will interfere and free Jerusalem from being trodden down by the Gentiles because their time has been fulfilled. No, God's wrath will last to the uttermost—to the end of the world—when the fullness of the Gentiles have come in, when Christ has come in glory to save "all Israel"—all faithful Jews and Gentiles—into His kingdom, while all sinners will be destroyed.

Looking at Jerusalem today, we notice that it is a city torn by the widely divided political and spiritual interests of Palestinians, Jews, Christians and Muslims. The city is unusually rich with synagogues, churches, monasteries and mosques. Various religions are represented in Jerusalem. For Muslims, it is a holy city because they believe, according to the Quran, that Muhammad came there in his Night Journey on a white horse and ascended to heaven from the place of the Al-Aqsa Mosque to speak with God. Jews and Christians have their own reasons for considering Jerusalem a holy city.

Jerusalem is not at all a city of peace. It has been destroyed a few times, besieged some 23 times, attacked more than 50 times, and captured or recaptured some 45 times.[23]

Although Jerusalem is in Jewish hands and the Jews are in the majority, we cannot, in all honesty, call the city, with its multicolored inhabitants, strictly a Jewish city. Statistics from 2011 show, in addition to Jews living in Jerusalem, that there were more than 281,000 Muslims, 14,000 Christians, and 9,000 persons of no specified religion.

---

23 http://1ref.us/bi, based on Eric H. Cline, *Jerusalem Besieged: From Ancient Canaan to Modern Israel* (Ann Arbor : University of Michigan Press, 2004), table 1, pp. 8–10.

Al-Aqsa Mosque in the Old City of Jerusalem

In 1967, the entire city of Jerusalem came under the control of the nation of Israel and was proclaimed their capital, though most countries did not recognize their claim, having regarded Tel Aviv to be Israel's capital. The international community also regards Israel's annexation of East Jerusalem illegal because it is Palestinian territory.

The Palestinians likewise claim Jerusalem as their capital, and they aim to make the whole city the confederate capital of the Palestinian State. The Jews have a similar goal, and many Israelis would like to clear away the Muslim's holy Temple Mount and rebuild in their place a third Jewish temple. This, however, would be a hazardous enterprise and would undoubtedly spark a furious battle, because this site is also regarded as holy by the Muslims. Militant Muslims make it no secret that it is their desire to return Israeli territory to Muslim control. Thus, there are extremely powerful conflicting interests that will always play a role in the city. Christians also see Jerusalem as a holy place, and their interests are also involved.

Jerusalem is a mixed city of many cultures. And even if Jerusalem were an actual Jewish city free of Gentiles, that would not be definite proof that Israel will be established again as God's chosen nation during a coming, earthly kingdom of peace and prosperity. After all, Jesus and the apostles never said a word about such an outcome. Rather, they have pictured the day of salvation as a present opportunity for all men, *before* the coming of Christ from on high, and not as an earthly hope that occurs after Jesus returns. Jesus said: "And when these things begin to come to pass, then look up, and lift up your heads; for your redemption draweth nigh" (Luke 21:28). So we are to look up to the heavens for our redemption and not down to Palestine to expect salvation there.

Jesus calls us to be alert and to watch and pray, for, otherwise, that great day may come to us like a trap. He said: "For as a snare shall it come on all them that dwell on the face of the whole earth. Watch ye therefore, and pray always, that ye may be accounted worthy to escape all these things that shall come to pass, and to stand before the Son of man" (Luke 21:35, 36). Jesus' statement clearly indicates everyone must prepare for His coming. It is an absolute necessity, for, if it is neglected, then that day will come upon us unexpectedly as a snare.

That thought certainly does not harmonize with the hope of being saved in an earthly kingdom. The words of Jesus are clear. No one on earth will escape the snare if they fail to prepare for that great day of the coming of Jesus. When He comes, it will be forever too late!

Part 3

Israel and the Old Testament

God's Covenant of Grace

When Adam and Eve fell into sin, God promised to put enmity between the serpent and the woman and between the serpent's seed and the woman's seed (Gen. 3:15).

The promised Seed, Jesus Christ, would, as the Lamb of God, conquer the powers of darkness to redeem humanity. By faithfully accepting the agreement of God's covenant of grace, human beings would receive power to resist the temptations of sin. However, the wickedness of humankind and the violence of humans and beasts increased. Therefore, God decided to destroy the earth, with man and beast, by a flood. Yet, Noah, a righteous man, found grace in the eyes of the Lord. God told Noah: "But with thee will I establish my covenant …" (Gen. 6:18). "And the Lord said unto Noah, Come thou and all thy house into the ark; for thee have I seen righteous before me in this generation" (Gen. 7:1). Thus, faithful Noah became the representative of God's covenant and was saved because he was righteous.

Some time after the flood, apostasy again gradually increased, and the knowledge of God was in danger of being forgotten. Then the Lord God called faithful Abraham and made His covenant of grace with him. God promised that Abraham would become a great and mighty nation and that all the nations of the earth would be blessed through him: "For I know him, that he will command his children and his household after him, and they shall keep the way of the Lord, to do justice and judgment; that the Lord may bring upon Abraham that which he hath spoken of him" (Gen. 18:19).

The Bible reveals that righteous living is the condition upon which rests the promises of God's covenant of grace. God spoke to Abraham: "I *am* the Almighty God; walk before me, and be thou perfect. And I will make my covenant between me and thee, and will multiply thee exceedingly.... As for me, behold, my covenant *is* with thee, and thou shalt be a father of many nations" (Gen. 17:1, 2, 4).

God put forth the condition upon which His covenant was to be established and fulfilled. He said: "Walk before me, and be perfect" (Gen. 17:1). The *New English Bible* says: "Live always in my presence and be perfect, so that I may set my covenant between myself and you and multiply your descendants" (Gen. 17:1, 2). God said: "As for me, behold, my covenant *is* with thee" (Gen. 17:4). God will always keep and fulfill His covenant, as long as its conditions are met. However, when righteous living ceases, God's covenant will no longer remain in effect. As long as people surrender their heart to the Spirit and perform their part faithfully, the promises and blessings of God's covenant will surely be theirs. We read that Abraham "believed in the Lord; and he counted it to him for righteousness" (Gen. 15:6). Then when Abraham was tested on Mount Moriah and exhibited unconditional trust in God, obeying His command, the angel of the Lord spoke God's blessing: "Now I know that you fear God ... because you have done this and have not withheld your son, your only son, I will surely bless you and make your descendants as numerous as the stars in the sky and as the sand on the seashore. Your descendants will take possession of the cities of their enemies, and through your offspring all nations on earth will be blessed, because you have obeyed me" (Gen. 22:12, 16–18, NIV). It cannot be denied that God established His covenant with Abraham *because of his faithful obedience.*

As long as people surrender their heart to the Spirit and perform their part faithfully, the promises and blessings of God's covenant will surely be theirs.

Abraham is called the father of all who believe, circumcised or not, who walk faithfully as he did (Rom. 4:11, 12). Nobody can deny that those who believe are in truth Abraham's children. However, should Abraham also be considered the father of his unfaithful descendants? Jesus gave a plain answer: "If ye were Abraham's children, ye would do the works of Abraham.... Ye are of *your* father the devil" (John 8:39, 44).

God gave the rite of circumcision as a sign of His covenant with Abraham and his seed, to emphasize the necessity and importance of inward purity and faithful obedience to God as a seal of righteousness (Gen. 17:11; Deut. 10:16; Rom. 4:11).

The Promised Land

Before the Israelites entered the Promised Land, Moses admonished them to love the Lord, to obey His voice and to walk in His ways. Through Moses, God set "life and death, blessing and cursing" before them to choose (Deut. 30:19). The Promised Land was intended to be theirs as a permanent possession. Nonetheless, if they served and worshiped other gods, Moses warned: "I tell you this day that you will perish; you will not live long in the land which you will enter to occupy after crossing the Jordan. I summon heaven and earth to witness against you this day: I offer you the choice of life and death, blessing or curse. Choose life and then you and your descendants will live; love the LORD your God, obey him and hold fast to him: that is life for you and length of days in the land which the LORD swore to give to your forefathers, Abraham, Isaac and Jacob" (Deut. 30:18–20, NEB). For God's part, there is absolute certainty, for God has sworn it! Yet, how is it on the human side? Is there also certainty? Can God indeed count on faith and obedience from His chosen people as their forefathers Abraham, Isaac and Jacob revealed? The Israelite's stay in the Promised Land is only secure if they walked in the way of the Lord.

The Israelite's stay in the Promised Land is only secure if they walked in the way of the Lord.

With faithful obedience they would dwell in the land that God gave to their fathers forever and ever (Jer. 7:3–7; Deut. 4:40; 5:32, 33). In unmistakable words, God repeatedly and emphatically reminded the Israelites that, as long as heaven and earth could be called to witness, if they were disobedient and did evil, they would "soon utterly perish from off the land ... ye shall not prolong *your* days upon it, but shall utterly be destroyed" (Deut. 4:26). What right does Israel have to regard the Promised Land as theirs when they live in unbelief and are unmindful of the Rock—Jesus Christ, the promised Messiah—who bore them, forgetting the God who gave them birth? (Deut. 32:18). The Bible prophesied that when God saw that they had forgotten their Rock, He "rejected," "spurned" and "abhorred" them (Deut. 32:19, AMP, NIV, ESV, KJV). "And he said, I will hide my face from them, I will see what their end *shall be*: for they *are* a very froward generation, children in whom *is* no faith. They have moved me to jealousy with *that which is* not God; they have provoked me to anger with their vanities: and I will move them to jealousy with *those which are* not a people; I will provoke them to anger with a foolish nation" (Deut. 32:20, 21). In no uncertain terms, Jesus declared that the kingdom would be taken from them and given to another nation (Matt. 21:43). Anyone who rejects the Rock Jesus Christ, the Stone who has become "the head of the corner," will feel its crushing weight upon him, and the Stone "will grind him to powder" (Matt. 21:42–44). Is this not clear indication that Israel forfeited the Promised Land as their possession?

Yet, should God's oath to Abraham, Isaac and Jacob regarding the Promised Land be understood as an indication that He will again restore Israel to Palestine in prosperity and peace?

We should remember that Israel's forefathers died without receiving the promise. They understood, however, the deeper significance, and they looked beyond the earthly Promised Land to a better country. They were strangers and pilgrims on this earth, and they longed for a heavenly country with a city built and prepared for them by God as the real fulfillment of His promise (Heb. 11:9–16). Since this is so, there is no basis for concluding that God has not kept His promise to them if He does not restore Israel as a converted and prosperous nation in Palestine.

God Doesn't Play Favorites

The promises of God's covenant that He confirmed with an oath will only be fulfilled when there is faith and obedience. He promised Abraham: "Sojourn in this land, and I will be with thee, and will bless thee ..." (Gen. 26:3). God truly fulfilled His promise, saying: "Because that Abraham obeyed my voice, and kept my charge, my commandments, my statutes, and my laws" (Gen. 26:5).

Then when Israel was gathered at Sinai, the divine message was: "Now therefore, if ye will obey my voice indeed, and keep my covenant, then ye shall be a peculiar treasure unto me above all people: for all the earth *is* mine: And ye shall be unto me a kingdom of priests, and an holy nation" (Exod. 19:5, 6). God's covenant with Israel is conditional.

Many people forget that the people of Israel's status as God's chosen, holy nation was dependent upon obedience. God said: "*If* you obey me ... *then* ... you will be my treasured possession ..." To this He added the very meaningful phrase, "for all the earth is mine" (Exod. 19:5, NIV, KJV). When the whole earth is God's property, then all people belong to God. But if God specially calls Israel His "peculiar treasure," or "treasured possession," does He not then favor Israel above other people? Should we conclude from this that God is partial? Jewish believer in Jesus Dr. Michael L. Brown writes:

> God will completely destroy other nations, but He will not completely destroy Israel! He treats His people differently from other people; they are judged more strictly, but they will never be wiped out. No matter what Israel does, God will never forsake them as a distinct people.[24]

When we consult the Scriptures and recognize them as our unfailing guide, we must agree that God is impartial in dealing with human beings. Moses described Him as "the awesome God, who is not partial" (Deut. 10:17, ESV). His statement could not be any more direct, and if it is true, then can He treat people very differently? Or will He not treat everybody equally without any distinction, giving them all similar chances and favors? That certainly is to be expected from a righteous God!

We should conclude then, if all people belong to God and He is not partial, but calls Israel His own special nation, that they undisputedly must comply with accordant conditions, whereby they are distinguished from other people and enter into a special relation to God. Otherwise, His impartiality would be at stake. We should also consider that such a special relation to God is not exclusively the prerogative of Israel but can be obtained by anyone who faithfully and obediently fulfills the conditions. This is precisely what the Scriptures stipulate.

---

24 Brown, *Our Hands Are Stained with Blood* (Shippensburg, PA: Destiny Image Publishers, 1990), p. 118.

If we look at the Bible text, in its context, that speaks about God's impartiality (Deut. 10:17), we will notice that the previous texts emphasize strict obedience: "And now, Israel, what doth the LORD thy God require of thee, but to fear the LORD thy God, to walk in all his ways, and to love him, and to serve the LORD thy God with all thy heart and with all thy soul, To keep the commandments of the LORD, and his statutes, which I command thee this day for thy good?" (vss. 12, 13). And then again, as in Exodus 19, Moses stressed that everything belongs to God: "Behold, the heaven and the heaven of heavens *is* the LORD's thy God, the earth *also*, with all that therein *is*" (Deut. 10:14). In the verse immediately following, the fathers of Israel are mentioned who obeyed and served God faithfully: "Only the LORD had a delight in thy fathers to love them, and he chose their seed after them, *even* you above all people, as *it is* this day" (Deut. 10:15). This special relation to God, above all people, requires, in fairness, special conditions. The following verse brings this out again clearly: "So circumcise [that is, remove sin from] your heart, and be stiff-necked (stubborn, obstinate) no longer" (Deut. 10:16, AMP). Only on this basis can Israel be truly and honestly God's elect and will His choice and impartiality be justified. Then the next verse says: "For the LORD your God is the God of gods and the Lord of lords, the great, the mighty, the awesome God who does not show partiality nor take a bribe" (Deut. 10:17, AMP). The following verse highlights God's justice—that He is not unmindful of the orphan and widow and that He loves the stranger: "He executes justice for the orphan and the widow, and shows His love for the stranger (resident alien, foreigner) by giving him food and clothing" (vs. 18, AMP). Once again, Moses stressed the conditions by which Israel would be God's elect: "Therefore, show your love for the stranger, for you were strangers in the land of Egypt. You shall fear [and worship] the LORD your God [with awe-filled reverence and profound respect]; you shall serve Him and cling to Him [hold tightly to Him, be united with Him], and you shall swear [oaths] by His name. He is your praise *and* glory; He is your God ..." (vss. 19–21, AMP).

This is saying that, if Israel did not meet the requirements of faithful obedience, God could not, because of His justice and impartiality, maintain her election as His special people. In light of Moses' statement, and the conditions it includes, can we legitimately say: "No matter what Israel does, God will never forsake them as a distinct people?"

If Israel wants to be God's distinct people, then it certainly matters what Israel does. Consider this biblical statement: "Therefore you shall keep the commandment, the statutes, and the judgments which I command you today, to observe them. 'Then it shall come to pass, because you listen to these judgments, and keep and do them, that the LORD your God will keep with you the covenant and the mercy which He swore to your fathers' " (Deut. 7:11, 12, NKJV). This passage clearly points out that only when Israel carefully followed God's laws, would the Lord keep His covenant and mercy with them as He swore to their fathers. However, if they walk in their own ways, God cannot, because of His justice and impartiality, keep His covenant with them. It follows that, without God's covenant and mercy, Israel will not be God's distinct people.

> *Only when Israel carefully followed God's laws, would the Lord keep His covenant and mercy with them as He swore to their fathers.*

So it definitely matters what Israel does. What they do clearly determines God's covenant and mercy with them. Only when they remember the Lord their God, can His covenant be established: "But thou shalt remember the LORD thy God ... that he may establish his covenant which he swore unto thy fathers, as *it is* this day" (Deut. 8:18).

When we look at the other part of the statement, is it biblically appropriate to say: "God will completely destroy other nations, but He will not completely destroy Israel! He treats His people differently from other people? ..."

Brown's appraisal alludes to God's promise in Jeremiah 30 and 46: "Though I completely destroy all the nations among which I scatter you, I will not completely destroy you. I will discipline you but only in due measure; I will not let you go entirely unpunished" (Jer. 30:11; 46:28, NIV). Both passages are in the context of the Babylonian captivity and Jeremiah's letter to the exiles, prophesying their return to their own land after seventy years. In that letter Jeremiah wrote: " 'Then you will call upon me and come and pray to me, and I will listen to you. You will seek me and find me *when you seek me with all your heart*. I will be found by you,' declares the LORD, 'and will bring you back from captivity ...' " (Jer. 29:12–14, NIV, emphasis supplied). Two verses before the promise used in Brown's appraisal, we read: "Instead, they will serve the LORD their God and David their king, whom I will raise up for them" (Jer. 30:9, NIV). Thus, within its context, the meaning of verse 11 becomes plain—Israel will not be completely destroyed as other nations, *because* they will seek the Lord and serve Him. Impartial justice demands that they be punished according to the sins that they have committed. There is no unrighteousness with God. He does not treat His people with partiality.

> *There is no unrighteousness with God. He does not treat His people with partiality.*

Moses had warned Israel before they entered the Promised Land: "If you ever forget the LORD your God and follow other gods and worship and bow down to them, I testify against you today that *you will surely be destroyed*. Like the nations the LORD destroyed before you, so you will be destroyed for not obeying the LORD your God" (Deut. 8:19, 20, NIV, emphasis added). These words are unambiguous. God does not treat His people differently from others. When they are disobedient, they will be destroyed—*just like the other nations*. All peoples of the earth belong to God, and He does not act arbitrarily for or against them. Rather, He takes action justly and without difference or respect of persons.

God is patient, and, in His goodness, He has given His wayward people many warnings and opportunities to repent and reform, but, once they have "filled up the measure" of their iniquity, He responds in justice and impartiality, punishing them the same way He punishes other disobedient people.

The "If" of God's Oath

It is amazing that many people cherish wrong views about Israel, even though the Bible, if carefully studied, quite clearly contradicts those ideas. Many people think that whatever may happen, Israel will always be God's elect because God has sworn it to the fathers, and He would not be the true God, if He would violate His oath. But these same people forget that the fulfillment of God's oath was conditioned upon their obedience.

We just cannot ignore the many times that God urgently commanded the children of Israel to walk in His ways and to carefully keep His statutes and commandments or that He predicated His promise of their being His peculiar people upon Israel's willing promise to obey Him. Thus, there is no doubt that Israel's obedience is absolutely the necessary condition of their being God's possession.

We find this conditionality clearly represented in the following Bible passages:

> Look down from Your holy habitation, from heaven, and bless Your people Israel and the land which You have given us, just as You swore to our fathers ... "This day the LORD your God commands you to observe these statutes and judgments; therefore you shall be careful to observe them with all your heart and with all your soul. Today you have proclaimed the LORD to be your God, and that you will walk in His ways and keep His statutes, His commandments, and His judgments, and that you will obey His voice. Also today the LORD has proclaimed you to be His special people, just as He promised you, that *you* should keep all His commandments, and that He will set you high above all nations which He has made, in praise, in name, and in honor, and that you may be a holy people to the LORD your God, just as He has spoken." (Deut. 26:15–19, NKJV)

And again we read:

> Now it shall be, if you diligently listen to *and* obey the voice of the LORD your God, being careful to do all of His commandments which I am commanding you today, the LORD your God will set you high above all the nations of the earth. ... The LORD will establish you as a people holy [and set apart] to Himself, just as He has sworn to you, if you keep the commandments of the LORD your God and walk [that is, live your life each and every day] in His ways. So all the peoples of the earth will see that you are called by the name of the LORD, and they will be afraid of you (Deut. 28:1, 9, 10, AMP).

The conditions are clear: Disobedience will result in doom; repentance will confirm God's covenant with the fathers. God swore that, if Israel were disobedient, they would be scattered among the heathen and the land would be desolated (Lev. 26:14, 32, 33). They would "perish among the heathen ..." (vs. 38). On the other hand,

He said, "If they shall confess their iniquity, and the iniquity of their fathers, ... if then their uncircumcised hearts be humbled, and they then accept of the punishment of their iniquity, ... then will I remember my covenant with Jacob ... Isaac ... and ... Abraham ... and I will remember the land" (vss. 40–42). This was particularly fulfilled after the Assyrian-Babylonian captivity.

Disobedience would undo the blessed oath that God swore to the fathers, and God would replace it, swearing another oath. Moses recorded: "And the LORD's anger was kindled the same time, and he sware, saying, Surely none of the men that came up out of Egypt, from twenty years old and upward, shall see the land which I sware unto Abraham, unto Isaac, and unto Jacob; because they have not wholly followed me" (Num. 32:10, 11).

God's oath of good, sworn to the fathers and the people, is clearly conditional: "The LORD shall establish thee an holy people unto himself, as he has sworn unto thee, **if** thou shalt keep the commandments of the LORD thy God, and walk in His ways" (Deut. 28:9, emphasis added).

Later, the word of the LORD came through Jeremiah saying: "Thus saith the LORD God of Israel; Cursed *be* the man that obeyeth not the words of this covenant, which I commanded your fathers ... saying, Obey my voice, and do them, according to all which I command you: so shall ye be my people, and I will be your God: **that I may perform the oath** which I have sworn unto your fathers, to give them a land flowing with milk and honey, as *it is* this day. Then answered I, and said, So be it, O LORD" (Jer. 11:3–5, emphasis added).

A comparison of some contemporary translations makes the conditional nature of God's message through Jeremiah even clearer. The *Tree of Life Version* says: "Listen to My voice, and do all that I command you. Then you will be My people, and I will be your God. Then I will fulfill the oath which I swore to your fathers ..." The *International Standard Version* reads: "Obey me and do everything that I commanded you. Then you will be my people and I'll be your God. As a result, I'll fulfill the oath that I made with your ancestors..." The *Complete Jewish Bible* says: "Listen to my voice, and carry out all my orders; then you will be my people, and I will be your God; so that I can fulfill the oath that I swore to your ancestors..." The *Message Bible* is even more to the point: "Your obedience will close the deal. You'll be mine and I'll be yours. This will provide the conditions in which I will be able to do what I promised your ancestors ..."

God's part of the covenant with His people is absolutely sure. He swore it with an oath. However, when His people break their part of the covenant by not meeting the conditions of faithful obedience, then God's impartial righteousness impedes His keeping His part of the covenant in blessing His people according to the promises sworn to their fathers. All the earth belongs to God. Because He is their Creator, all people are equally His (cf. Amos 9:7). If God should perform the blessings of His covenant to a wayward, unfaithful and disobedient people, then the other nations would have a case to testify against God in that they were rejected because of their unbelief and disobedience. Would not Satan also have reason to accuse God, for he was thrown out of heaven because of his unfaithfulness. Did God somehow walk into a trap when He swore His oath of blessing to the fathers? No, not at all, for He made it crystal clear that obedience was the condition upon which God would keep His covenant oath (cf. Gen. 17:1-9; 18:19; 26:3-5).

God's promises are without repentance as long as the conditions for receiving them are met (cf. Gen. 6:5, 6; Rom. 11:22, 29). Those who maintain that God will always keep His promises to Israel, even if they continue in disobedience, are painting their Creator as being partial and unjust.

> *God's condition on which He will be able to fulfill to Israel His oath, sworn to their fathers, is impartial and applies to every human being alike.*

God, however, does not act similarly like Jacob did, who loved and favored his son Joseph more than all his children. This unjust, preferential treatment caused disharmony and much displeasure in Jacob's family (Gen. 37:3, 4). God's condition on which He will be able to fulfill to Israel His oath, sworn to their fathers, is impartial and applies to every human being alike. He will not reject any upright man but bless and sustain all those who are loyal to Him (Cf. Deut. 30:9, 10; 1 Sam. 12:24, 25; 2 Chron. 16:9; Ezra 8:22b; Job 8:20; Psalms 1:1-3). He deals with other people and individuals just the same way as He treats the children of Israel. Their kings, although chosen by God, were not dealt with differently either, if they continued in disobedience. God rejected king Saul, because he rejected the word of the Lord (1 Sam. 15:23; 16:1). King Solomon was admonished: "If you seek Him, He will be found by you; but if you forsake Him, He will cast you off forever" (1 Chron. 28:9 NKJV). And so, accordingly, because God's people continued in their disobedience and wickedness, the prophet Hosea prophesied: "My God will reject them *and* cast them away Because they did not listen to Him; And they will be wanderers (fugitives) among the nations" (Hosea 9:17 AMP).

Thus, the Bible indicates, beyond dispute, that Israel's response and Israel's actions matter. They determine whether God will establish His people as His holy elect, since His oath was predicated on Israel's obedience. Many Bible passages clearly indicate that, among many other things, obedience or disobedience determines the difference between blessings and curses (Deut. 28:2, 45; 11:26–28), between life and death (Deut. 30:15, 19), and between prosperity and destruction (Deut. 29:9; 28:11, 20, 29, 63).

Blessings or Curses

Now notice what will happen to the man who thinks lightly of the curses that God made known to Israel and continues to walk in his own way, expecting that he will still be blessed and have peace:

> And it come to pass, when he heareth the words of this curse, that he bless himself in his heart, saying, I shall have peace, though I walk in the imagination of mine heart, to add drunkenness to thirst: The LORD will not spare him, but then the anger of the LORD and his jealousy shall smoke against that man, and all the curses that are written in this book shall lie upon him, and the LORD shall blot out his name from under heaven. And the LORD shall separate him unto evil out of all the tribes of Israel, according to all the curses of the covenant that are written in this book of the law (Deut. 29:19–21).

This is not an unimportant matter. Moses describes that which will be the lot of the man who thinks lightly of the curses and believes that he will still be blessed.

There are many people even now who exhibit, like this man, a flippant attitude about God's favor for Israel. They do not count on the curses but declare that Israel will always be God's blessed elect—no matter what they do. God certainly would never forsake His chosen people—they proclaim loudly—Israel will, in the end, be a blessed, prosperous and peaceful nation. Yet, those who proclaim such things are on a collision course with disappointment because God is faithful in all His promises.

God is indeed long-suffering. Yet, once a person or a nation reaches the limit of insolence before God, then God will surely act. The prophet Jeremiah lived during the critical period before and during the Babylonian captivity. Because of Israel's continued disobedience and persistent violation of God's covenant, they forfeited their right to the Promised Land, and God forsook His house and heritage and gave His people into the hands of their enemies (Jer. 12:7). When the ten tribes were led into Assyrian captivity in 722 BC, the kingdom of Judah did not learn their lesson, nor did they repent of their wicked ways. Notice that Jeremiah addressed his divine message of doom not only to wicked Judah but also to the wicked surrounding nations—they would all be uprooted from their lands. God deals fairly with all people. Jeremiah declared:

> Thus says the LORD concerning all my evil neighbors who touch the heritage that I have given my people Israel to inherit: "Behold, I will pluck them up from their land, and I will pluck up the house of Judah from among them. And after I have plucked them up, I will again have compassion on them, and I will bring them again each to his heritage and each to his land. And it shall come to pass, if they will diligently learn the ways of my people, to swear by my name, 'As the LORD lives,' even as they taught my people to swear by Baal, then they shall be built up in the midst of my people. But if any nation will not listen, then I will utterly pluck it up and destroy it, declares the LORD." (Jer. 12:14–17, ESV)

God is gracious in offering second chances, but when people turn back to their wickedness, He has frankly declared that He will utterly pluck them up and destroy them.

As an object lesson for the people, Jeremiah was ordered to retrieve his belt, or girdle, that he had hidden for many days in the hole of a rock. It had become marred and useless (Jer. 13:4–7). God's intended message from this was:

"In the same way I will ruin the pride of Judah and the great pride of Jerusalem. These wicked people, who refuse to listen to my words, who follow the stubbornness of their hearts and go after other gods to serve and worship them, will be like this belt—completely useless! For as a belt is bound around the waist, so I bound all the people of Israel and all the people of Judah to me," declares the Lord, "to be my people for my renown and praise and honor. But they have not listened." ...

"This is what the Lord says: I am going to fill with drunkenness all who live in this land, including the kings who sit on David's throne, the priests, the prophets and all those living in Jerusalem. I will smash them one against the other, parents and children alike, declares the Lord. I will allow no pity or mercy or compassion to keep me from destroying them." (Jer. 13:9–11, 13, 14, NIV).

If once the limit is reached, God will no longer be gracious, although He will always spare the faithful remnant.

Probationary Time

After the Assyrian-Babylonian captivity, God was still merciful with His people and promised to turn again to Israel and restore them to the Promised Land. As He had promised, God did not, at that time, make a "full end" of them (Jer. 5:18). He revealed to the prophet Daniel: "Seventy weeks [of years, or 490 years] have been decreed for your people and for your holy city (Jerusalem), to finish the transgression ..." (Dan. 9:24, AMP).

Jerusalem, King David Monument

The *Common English Bible* says: "Seventy weeks are appointed for your people and for your holy city to complete the rebellion …"

This prophetic period, specifically measured for Israel and Jerusalem, with a day representing a year (cf. Ezek. 4:6), ends during the time of Christ, when the Jews were to either finish their transgression or bring it to completion, filling the cup, or "measure," of their iniquity to the brim (cf. Matt. 23:32).

The angel messenger told Daniel when the beginning event of this special period would be: "So you are to know and understand that from the issuance of the command to restore and rebuild Jerusalem until [the coming of] the Messiah (the Anointed One), the Prince, *there will be* seven weeks [of years] and sixty-two weeks [of years] …" (Dan. 9:25, AMP).

Three rulers of the Medo-Persian empire issued decrees toward the restoration of Israel. The third of these, issued in 457 BC, the seventh year of king Artaxerxes, dealt with the complete restoration of Israel and Jerusalem as a religious and civil state.[25] This makes 457 BC the correct year to start the period of the seventy weeks, or 490 years, allotted to Jewish Israel to complete their rebellion and fill up the measure of their fathers (Matt. 23:32). With this starting point, it is easy to determine that the end of this appointed period of grace for Israel was at hand in the days of Jesus and to calculate that it reached its completion in the year 34 AD. No wonder Jesus wept over Jerusalem when they did not know what would bring them peace nor recognize the time of God's graceful visitation (Luke 19:42–44). Jesus declared to the unwilling leaders of the Jews that the kingdom would be taken from them (Matt. 21:43) and that their house would be left unto them desolate (Matt. 23:38). These words, as the words of Jesus, are trustworthy and in full harmony with the words of the prophets.

If Israel walked in their own ways and the allotted time period passed fruitlessly without obedience, faith and repentance, then they were to be blotted out as God's holy nation.

---

25   For confirmation of this date, see Gleason L. Archer, *Encyclopedia of Bible Difficulties* (Grand Rapids, MI: Zondervan Publishing House, 1982), p. 290.

Moses declared that the man who thinks he will still be blessed while continuing to walk in his own ways, will not be spared. Rather, he will be cursed and his name blotted out (Deut. 29:19–21). This was not meant to be an incidental case but was intended as a lesson for everyone. If Israel walked in their own ways and the allotted time period passed fruitlessly without obedience, faith and repentance, then they were to be blotted out as God's holy nation.

The allotted time period of grace in the days of Noah was 120 years, but when this period passed by without repentance and reformation, the flood came as predicted and all the rebellious perished (Gen. 6:3, 13; 7:23).

God told Abraham: "Then in the fourth generation your descendants shall return here [to Canaan, the land of promise], for the wickedness *and* guilt of the Amorites is not yet complete (finished)" (Gen. 15:16, AMP).

Before Israel crossed the river Jordan, Moses told the Israelites that it was because of the wickedness of the nations that they were to be driven out (Deut. 9:4). These nations were very sinful and did detestable things. God declared: "Even the land was defiled; so I punished it for its sin, and the land vomited out its inhabitants" (Lev. 18:25, NIV). Israel was warned: "And if you defile the land, it will vomit you out as it vomited out the nations that were before you" (Lev. 18:28, NIV).

God is gracious and longsuffering towards all people, but once they have filled the cup of their iniquity, He will deal with them equally, and the people of Israel will not be treated as an exception. They will be punished just as any other nation.

When Israel worshiped the golden calf at Sinai, God's wrath was raised hot. Of their number, approximately three thousand men were killed (Exod. 32:28). But those who were on the Lord's side were separated from the rebellious and spared (vs. 26).

When the twelve spies were sent to search out the land and then came back, forty days later, ten of the spies distrusted God and brought back an evil report of the land. And all the Israelites wept, complained and rebelled. As a result, God proclaimed that they would all, from twenty years upward, perish in the wilderness, except for Joshua and Caleb, the two spies who trusted God and encouraged the people to go in and possess the land. They were assured that they would enter the land (Num. 13:2; 14:6–9, 28–38).

Another example of the impartiality of God's justice in dealing with wicked people—whether Jews or Gentiles—was the rebellion of

Korah and his sympathizers, who perished alive as the earth swallowed them. Even with that example before them, because the seeds of rebellion had been sown, another fourteen thousand seven hundred people of Israel were destroyed in rebellion (Num. 16:32, 49).

Just before Israel entered the Promised Land, they committed adultery with Moab's daughters and practiced idolatry. The Lord was angry with them and sent a plague that claimed the lives of the guilty multitude of twenty-four thousand souls. And so we see clearly that God does not spare His people if they do evil. He deals justly with them as He does with other people, and He does not slay the righteous with the wicked. As Abraham protested when God told Him about the impending destruction of Sodom and Gomorrah: "Far be it from You to do such a thing as this, to slay the righteous with the wicked, so that the righteous should be as the wicked; far be it from You! Shall not the Judge of all the earth do right?" (Gen. 18:25, NKJV).

The prophet Jeremiah predicted manifold judgments over the Jews. They were to be cast out of God's sight and delivered to death, the sword, famine and captivity because they had forsaken their God and gone backward. Therefore, the Lord, weary with repenting of His promised judgment, would stretch out His hand against them and destroy them. Because they did not return from their ways, God would destroy His people (Jer. 15:1–10). Notice how God, amidst the threat of severe judgments, comforts His faithful remnant: "The LORD said, Verily it shall be well with thy remnant; verily I will cause the enemy to entreat thee *well* in the time of evil and in the time of affliction" (vs. 11).

Thus we see that God deals justly with humankind. He is gracious towards all those in Israel who are not overcome by sin, and He treats other people the same way. He does not treat any differently.

The people that were driven out before Israel were not all destroyed. Israel was to follow God's instructions, and God would fight for Israel. When Israel came to distant cities to attack, peace was to be offered, and, if the people would accept their offer and open the gates, they could be spared and be Israel's servants (Deut. 20:4, 10, 11; cf. Josh. 11:18–23).

Among the nations that God commanded to be totally destroyed, not any creature was to be left alive. These were the Hittites, Amorites, Canaanites and the Jebusites (Deut. 20:17). Nonetheless, there were some exceptions among them—apparently because certain people showed some faith in the God of Israel. Everywhere among the nations there are often a few who are honest of heart and desirous of light and knowledge to live a better life, and God is not unmindful of them. His eyes "run to and fro throughout the whole earth" to strengthen them "whose heart *is* perfect toward him" (2 Chron. 16:9). God will not permit any soul to perish who longs to live a righteous, better life. Accordingly, not all the wicked nations were destroyed. The temple of Solomon, for instance, was built on the threshing floor of the Jebusite Araunah, or Ornan (2 Sam. 24:18; 2 Chron. 3:1). In the genealogy of Jesus Christ, we find two Canaanitish women, Thamar, daughter-in-law of Judah, and Rahab, the harlot of Jericho (Matt. 1:3, 5). Rahab showed faith in God, hiding the spies of Israel. For her faith and assistance, she was saved alive with all those with her in her house (Josh. 2:11–19; 6:17, 25). Among the heroes of David were several men from other nations, including the Hittite Uriah (2 Sam. 23:39), whose wife Bathsheba, was treacherously taken by David. Matthew mentions the wife of Uriah in his genealogy of Jesus (Matt. 1:6). Thus, there is some clear evidence that the guilty, wicked nations were not totally destroyed; those among them of good will were graciously spared.

Twofold Messages

Some people are puzzled because the prophets speak of doom and destruction and, at the same time, of hope, blessing and prosperity. Many people are inclined to neglect the disastrous messages and focus on the hopeful ones, and they loudly proclaim that God will certainly fulfill all that He has promised.

It should be noted, however, that, while the determined period of grace continued, it is understandable that the messages of the prophets would be two-sided. On the one hand, they delivered warning messages of death and ruin, and, on the other hand, they delivered graceful messages of recovery and peace, together with calls to repent and obey the Lord.

Consider the word of the Lord that came to the prophet Jeremiah:

> "At one moment I might [suddenly] speak concerning a nation or kingdom, that I will uproot and break down and destroy; if that nation against which I have spoken turns from its evil, I will relent *and* reverse My decision concerning the devastation that I intended to do. Or at another time I might [suddenly] speak about a nation or kingdom that I will build up or establish; and if they do evil in My

sight by not obeying My voice, then I will reverse My decision concerning the good with which I had promised to bless them. Now then, say to the men of Judah and to the citizens of Jerusalem, 'Thus says the LORD, "Behold, I am shaping a disaster and working out a plan against you. Turn back, each of you from his evil way; correct your habits and change your actions for the better." ' " (Jer. 18:7–11, AMP)

Thus, what Israel chooses to do is extremely important. If God promises recovery in building and planting Israel, but they do evil and do not obey His voice, then He will reverse His decision and the promised blessing will be withheld. To many people's surprise, the result of conditionality in prophecy is that many scriptural prophecies are left unfulfilled. One such example is God's message to the people of Nineveh by the prophet Jonah. He preached: "Yet forty days, and Nineveh shall be overthrown," but the people of Nineveh believed God and repented, and God's judgment was not fulfilled. God saw "… that they turned from their evil way; and God repented of the evil, that he had said that he would do unto them; and he did *it* not" (Jonah 3:10).

Another example is king Hezekiah's sickness. The prophet Isaiah brought the king God's message that he would die. However, the king prayed earnestly to God, and Isaiah returned to him with the message that God had heard his prayer and that he would not die but would live fifteen more years (2 Kings 20:1–6).

God's message concerning Jerusalem was that it would be prosperous and would remain forever if Israel would faithfully keep the Sabbath. However, if they would not be obedient nor hallow the Sabbath, then Jerusalem would be destroyed by fire. Because of Israel's disobedience, the first prediction was not fulfilled. The second one was: the city was destroyed by fire by the Babylonian army, and many were taken captive to Babylon (Jer. 17:24–27; 2 Chron. 36:19).

The prophecies and promises of God are absolutely sure. Yet, for them to be fulfilled requires a willing and obedient heart.

The prophecies and promises of God are absolutely sure. Yet, for them to be fulfilled requires a willing and obedient heart. The

Lord's hand is never shortened that it cannot save, and His ear is not dull that it cannot hear, but iniquities can cause a separation so that God does not hear (Isa. 59:1–3).

God's message was that the people of Israel had a rebellious heart. They did not say, "Let us now fear the LORD our God, that giveth rain, both the former and the latter, in his season: he reserveth unto us the appointed weeks of the harvest. Your iniquities have turned away these *things*, and your sins have withholden good *things* from you" (Jer. 5:24, 25). Therefore, Israel's iniquities are the reason that God's good blessings and promises are withheld or are fulfilled only in a restricted way.

We must be very careful about the predictions of the ancient prophets concerning Israel and not come to wrong conclusions. If the conditions are not met because of disobedience, then the prophecies may not be literally fulfilled for Israel or may be only partially fulfilled, or they may be fulfilled in some sense for spiritual Israel.

A Plan for All the Faithful

The Bible teaches us that God's Spirit will not always strive with humankind when they live in sin: "Then the LORD said, 'My Spirit shall not strive *and* remain with man forever, because he is indeed flesh [sinful, corrupt—given over to sensual appetites] …' " (Gen. 6:3, AMP).

These words were not intended for the people who lived before the Flood alone; they apply to all people—including the children of Israel. Whenever there is renewed and recalcitrant unbelief and wickedness, God's Spirit will eventually cease to strive with impenitent Israel and will withdraw from them, as He would do with any other nation. Israel's time of probation lasted from the Assyrian-Babylonian captivity until the time that the Son of God came as Israel's promised Messiah.

It was the prophet Amos who established, a number of years before the Assyrian captivity, that Israel, while living in sin, should not think that they were particularly privileged above other nations. We read: " 'Are not you Israelites the same to me as the Cushites?' declares the LORD. 'Did I not bring Israel up from Egypt, the Philistines from Caphtor and the Arameans from Kir?' " (Amos 9:7, NIV).

If Israel is the same to God as other nations, should we expect God to treat Israel any differently? If God would treat them differently, tolerating sin among the Jews that He would not tolerate among others, then Israel is not the same. However, as Scripture declares, God does not make a difference. All people are to Him the same. If Israel lives in sin, then they are the same to God as any other sinful nation. Amos continues:

> "Behold, the eyes of the Lord GOD are on the sinful [northern] kingdom [of Israel's ten tribes] and I shall destroy it from the face of the earth; but I shall not totally destroy the house of Jacob [that is, the entire nation of Israel]," says the LORD. "For behold, I am commanding, and I shall shake *and* sift the house of Israel among all nations [and cause it to tremble] like *grain* is shaken in a sieve [removing the chaff], but not a kernel [of the faithful remnant] shall fall to the ground *and* be lost [from My sight]. All the sinners among My people will die by the sword, those who say [defiantly], 'The disaster will not overtake or confront us.'" (Amos 9:8–10, AMP)

Notice that he declares that the sinners in Israel will die. He gives no indication that there is any hope of their coming back in an earthly millennial kingdom to be converted and to serve the Lord their God. There is, however, hope of a different sort. Israel will not be totally destroyed but will be sifted; the rebels will die, and the faithful remnant will be saved.

Amos continues his prophetic message concerning Israel's restoration: "'On that day I will raise up the tabernacle of David, which has fallen down, and repair its damages; I will raise up its ruins, and rebuild it as in the days of old; that they may possess the remnant of Edom [Septuagint reads *mankind*], and all the Gentiles who are called by My name,' says the LORD who does this thing" (Amos 9:11, 12, NKJV).

Israel will be built up again and then the remnant of Edom—that is, mankind and all Gentiles called by the name of the Lord—*will be part of Israel*. Isaiah, similarly, prophesied that Israel's "seed shall inherit the Gentiles, and make the desolate cities to be inhabited" (Isa. 54:3). Thus we see that the fallen tabernacle of David will be built and raised up by a faithful remnant through believing Gentiles. This is precisely what was affirmed by the apostle James in the assembly at Jerusalem:

> "Therefore I will return and rebuild the fallen house of David; even from its ruins I will rebuild it, and set it up again, that they may seek the Lord—all the rest of man-

kind, and the Gentiles, whom I have claimed for my own. Thus says the Lord, whose work it is, made known long ago" (Acts 15:13–18, NEB).

The prophet Amos further prophesies: " 'I will bring back the captives of My people Israel; they shall build the waste cities and inhabit *them*; they shall plant vineyards and drink wine from them; they shall also make gardens and eat fruit from them. I will plant them in their land, and no longer shall they be pulled up from the land I have given them,' says the LORD your God" (Amos 9:14, 15, NKJV).

At the close of the seventy years of captivity, Israel was, by God's grace, brought back to the Promised Land to build it up again, and, if they would then be obedient and serve their God, they would no longer be uprooted from the land that God gave them. But Israel failed again to walk in God's ways and to obey His voice. Therefore, the promised recovery was only partially fulfilled as they went on to fill up the cup of their iniquity in rejecting their Messiah.

In looking at the context of the message that Amos proclaimed, it seems justified to suggest that this predicted return might also find a further, complete fulfillment when the earth is made new. The prediction of Amos is that David's fallen tabernacle will be raised and built up by believing Gentiles, making Israel a composite of a faithful Jewish remnant and believing Gentiles. As we have noted, all the faithful worthies of old died "not having received the promises ... and confessed that they were strangers and pilgrims on the earth" (Heb. 11:13; cf. Psa. 119:19). They could do this because they were looking for a better, heavenly country with a city prepared for them by God (Heb. 11:10, 16).

This heavenly city, the New Jerusalem, will come down from God out of heaven, and God's heavenly kingdom will be established on the earth made new. God promises a new heaven and a new earth (Rev. 21:1, 2), and all Israel—all the faithful Jews and all believing Gentiles—will inherit the promised "better country" that the faithful worthies of old anticipated.

Therefore, Amos prophesied in harmony with the teaching of the Scriptures, "I will plant them in their land, and no longer shall they be pulled up from the land I have given them" (Amos 9:15, NKJV). God has given the earth to the children of humanity (Ps. 115:16). God's eternal plan and promise, sworn to the fathers, will then be forever gloriously fulfilled. Listen to the words of John the Revelator as he describes the glorious fulfillment:

> And I heard a loud voice from heaven saying, "Behold, the tabernacle of God *is* with men, and He will dwell with them, and they shall be His people. God Himself will be with them *and be* their God. And God will wipe away every tear from their eyes; there shall be no more death, nor sorrow, nor crying. There shall be no more pain, for the former things have passed away." (Rev. 21:3, 4, NKJV)

After the millennium, the new earth with the heavenly city, the New Jerusalem, will be the long-awaited abode of eternal bliss for the saints of all the ages.

Scattered and Dispersed

Because God's promises regarding Israel's recovery from the Assyrian-Babylonian captivity had only a limited fulfillment in the return of a portion of the Jews, many people reason that the prophets had still another return of Israel in mind at the end of time. They emphasize that, since the prophets speak of a large-scale dispersion of Israel and Judah among many nations with a return from all the lands to which God scattered them "toward every wind" (Ezek. 12:14), that the recovery that took place after the Assyrian-Babylonian captivity was too limited to fulfill the predicted gathering from so many nations, countries and "every wind." Thus, they believe that the prophets must have looked beyond Israel's return in the past to a more massive gathering of Israel in the future in which Israel will be converted and accept the rejected Messiah. They picture a restored, bright and mighty nation at peace that will be a channel of blessing among the nations during the Messiah's Millennial Kingdom. However, such reasoning goes beyond what the Bible indicates about Israel's recovery and return from the Assyrian-Babylonian captivity.

The prophet Ezekiel prophesied that the prince in Jerusalem and all the house of Israel will go into exile and captivity. He declared that the prince would die in Babylon. He described the dismay of all the prince's supporters: "I will scatter to every wind all who are around him, his helpers and all his troops; and I will draw out a sword after them. So they will know *and* understand fully that I am the Lord when I scatter them among the nations and disperse them among the [pagan] countries" (Ezek. 12:14, 15, AMP).

Thus, we see that, with the Babylonian captivity, the people of Israel were to be scattered to every wind, dispersed among the countries. The emphasis of this prophecy does not indicate another return beyond their return from the Babylonian captivity. When the prophecy was fulfilled, and Israel was led into captivity, God said: "Also I scattered them among the nations and they were dispersed throughout the countries. I judged *and* punished them in accordance with their conduct and their [idolatrous] behavior" (Ezek. 36:19, AMP).

The dispersion of Israel among the nations was completed in the days of Ezekiel, and it is unwarranted to project another dispersion at a much later date from these words, applying them to it a return at the end of time, when the Scriptures are silent on such further reasoning. God's promised return is explicit: "When seventy years are completed for Babylon, I will come to you and fulfill my good promise to bring you back to this place" (Jer. 29:10, NIV). The anticipated return to the Promised Land was to bring them home from the Babylonian captivity. The prophecy continues: " 'I will be found by you,' declares the LORD, 'and will bring you back from captivity. I will gather you from all the nations and places where I have banished you,' declares the LORD, 'and will bring you back to the place from which I carried you into exile' " (vs. 14). Thus, Israel's return from all the lands to which they were scattered is unmistakably described in Scripture as a return from the captivity *at that time*, without any reference to another future gathering in the time of the end.

When we consider that Assyria and Babylon were, during the period of Israel's captivity, both mighty nations that ruled lands and peoples that bought and sold people from conquered lands as slaves, then we should not be surprised that some of the Jewish exiles were dispersed to many nations and lands. The prophet Joel says: "You sold the people of Judah and Jerusalem to the Greeks, that you might send them far from their homeland" (Joel 3:6, NIV). The prophet Ezekiel also speaks of human beings that were traded: "Greece, Tubal and Meshek did business with you; they traded human beings and articles of bronze for your wares" (Ezek. 27:13, NIV).

The prophet Jeremiah also informs us that, during the period of Israel's captivity, a number of Jews went to Egypt against the word of the Lord (Jer. 43:6, 7). Most of them, however, perished by the sword or from famine. Yet, some did survive and return to their homeland (Jer. 44:11–14, 28).

Thus, it is clear that Israel and Judah at the time of their Assyrian-Babylonian captivity were dispersed and scattered to every wind, to many nations and lands and that the promised return had to do with this same captivity.

Another Return?

The following promise of God merits our attention: " 'Thus says the LORD of hosts: Behold, I will save my people from the east country and from the west country, and I will bring them to dwell in the midst of Jerusalem. And they shall be my people, and I will be their God, in faithfulness and in righteousness' " (Zech. 8:7, 8, ESV).

Since God gave this promise when the return from Babylonian captivity had taken place and the foundation of the temple at Jerusalem had already been laid, should we see Zechariah's prophecy as representing another, future return apart from the captivity? Many people proclaim so. Yet, we must be careful about jumping to conclusions. We should consider that not everyone returned from the lands to which they were dispersed as the seventy-year term passed. Only a rather small group returned. Many of the scattered did not respond to the call to return. No wonder the prophets sought to encourage more of those in captivity to return by repeating God's promises of saving His people from the different countries and bringing them back to Jerusalem. The return from the scattering of Babylon and Assyria spanned a rather long period of time. The first group returned in 536 BC under Zerubbabel. Several years later, in 457 BC, another group returned under Ezra, and, some years later, in 444 BC, Nehemiah arrived in Jerusalem with yet another group.

Zechariah's prophecy (circa 520 BC) came when the first return under Zerubbabel had taken place some sixteen years before. The return under Ezra would not take place for another 63 years. Thus, it is understandable that the prophet Zechariah, under inspiration, would bring messages of hope and encouragement to stimulate a further return from the Babylonian-Assyrian captivity.

If we read the book of Zechariah carefully, we will notice that the prophet had no other return in mind and that his messages were focused on those who had not yet returned.

If we read the book of Zechariah carefully, we will notice that the prophet had no other return in mind and that his messages were focused on those who had not yet returned. For example, we read: "I will whistle for them and gather them in, for I have redeemed them, and they shall be as many as they were before. Though I scattered them among the nations, yet in far countries they shall remember me, and with their children they shall live and return. I will bring them home from the land of Egypt, and gather them from Assyria ..." (Zech. 10:8–10, ESV).

In the last chapters of his prophecy, Zechariah predicted manifold blessings for Israel. However, because of Israel's unfaithfulness, these prophecies could not be literally fulfilled. They may, however, find a partial fulfillment in spiritual Israel.

The prophets of old proclaimed messages of triumph and hope as well as messages of punishment and judgment. The prophet Habakkuk prophesied the coming of the Babylonian forces against the apostate kingdom of Judah (Hab. 1:5–7). Yet, he promises that, amidst judgment and affliction, God's faithful children will not die (vs. 12). The righteous, he declares, will live by his faith (Hab. 2:4).[26]

The prophet Zephaniah also predicted impending doom and destruction for Israel because of their continued apostasy. Looking beyond the judgments of their days, he also addresses the apostate world of the last days at the coming of Christ, when, in the "great day of the Lord," all the wicked and impenitent sinners will be utterly consumed and no human being or animal will be left (Zeph. 1:1–18).

Nonetheless, the prophet also speaks of a bright hope: "At that time I will deal with all who oppressed you. I will rescue the lame; I will gather the exiles. I will give them praise and honor in every land where they have suffered shame" (Zeph. 3:19, NIV).

It is clear that this message of hope and return is in reference to the period of Israel's captivity. The prophet continues: "At that time will I bring you *again*, even in the time that I gather you: for I will make you a name and a praise among all people of the earth, when I turn back your captivity before your eyes, saith the LORD" (Zeph. 3:20, KJV).

This prophecy was realized after the captivity. The returned exiles finally made a name for themselves by their united work, and they were praised when they finished Jerusalem's wall in just fifty-two days. All the nations were filled with fear because they recognized in this wonderful achievement that God was with His people and that

---

26   In Romans 1:17; Galatians 3:11; and Hebrews 10:38, Paul showcased this promise within the context of the new covenant.

their prosperous work was accomplished with His gracious intervention, help and guidance (Neh. 6:15, 16).

With this understanding, there is no reason for a further fulfillment in the last days, as some people expect, of Israel's becoming a glorious, converted nation with the Messiah as their Millennial King on David's throne.

"Last Days" Already in the Past

Many call attention to a prediction of Hosea in which they discern Israel's last-day return to the Lord. The prophecy to which they refer reads: "For the children of Israel shall dwell many days without king or prince, without sacrifice or pillar, without ephod or household gods. Afterward the children of Israel shall return and seek the LORD their God, and David their king, and they shall come in fear to the LORD and to his goodness in the latter days" (Hosea 3:4, 5, ESV).

Is this not a clear indication, they assert, that in the *"last days,"* as some Bibles have it, Israel will seek the Lord? Does Hosea not clearly indicate here that Israel, in the last days, will be a blessed nation with the Messiah as their king on David's throne in His millennial kingdom? We would respond: Does Hosea's message even speak to these issues?

Nobody questions whether the prophets of old delivered timely messages for the circumstances in which they lived. In the time of Ezekiel, people tried to ease their conscience by interpreting the vision of Ezekiel as being for many years in the future (Ezek. 12:27). Yet, the word of the Lord came through Ezekiel declaring: "For I *am* the LORD: I will speak, and the word that I shall speak shall come to pass; it shall be no more prolonged: for in your days, O rebellious house, will I say the word, and will perform it, saith the Lord GOD.... Therefore say unto them, Thus saith the Lord GOD; There shall none of my words be prolonged any more, but the word which I have spoken shall be done, saith the Lord GOD" (vss. 25, 28).

He said the fulfillment would come "in your days" and indicated that "it shall be no more prolonged." We mislead ourselves if we choose to overlook the direct meaning of the prophets concerning the original time and circumstances of their messages. To correctly understand their messages, we need to ask: *When* did the prophet live, and *what was the situation* at the time he proclaimed his message?

In the book of Hosea, there are sufficient historical clues for us to determine that Hosea lived in the eight century BC and that he prophesied in the northern kingdom. The situation when he preached was not very favorable. The division of Israel in two—with ten tribes in the northern kingdom of Israel and in two tribes in the southern kingdom of Judah—had taken place a number of years before. The description of Hosea in his prophecy answers precisely to the situation of his day. Back when the kingdom had divided, the ten tribes had a king but not from God's chosen house of David. When the Assyrians deported a great number of the people from their country, Israel went without a king or a prince for a long time.

Because of their rebellion against Judah, the northern kingdom of Israel was separated from Jerusalem's royal throne of David and from the beautiful temple of Solomon, which was the place of God's salvation and grace. Subsequently, the kingdom of Israel existed for a long time without sacrifice, ephod, teraphim or other religious emblems. After this time of spiritual void, according to the prophet Hosea, the people were to return and seek the Lord their God and David their king. Is this what actually happened at that time?

It was king Hezekiah who sent word to all Israel and Judah inviting them to come to the temple in Jerusalem and celebrate the Passover. Couriers went throughout all Israel and Judah with the royal message. Though the couriers were ridiculed in some places, many, many people accepted the invitation.

> A very large crowd of people assembled in Jerusalem to celebrate the Feast of Unleavened Bread ... The Israelites who were present in Jerusalem celebrated the Feast of Unleavened Bread for seven days with great rejoicing ... For the seven days they ate their assigned portion and offered fellowship offerings and praised the LORD, the God of their fathers. The whole assembly then agreed to celebrate the festival seven more days; so for another seven days they celebrated joyfully.... The entire assembly of Judah rejoiced, along with the priests and Levites and all who had assembled from Israel, including the aliens who had come from Israel and those who lived in Judah. There was great joy in Jerusalem, for since the days of Solomon son of David king of Israel there had been nothing like this in Jerusalem. The priests and the Levites stood to bless the people, and God heard them, for their prayer reached heaven, his holy dwelling place. (2 Chron. 30:13, 21–23, 25–27, NIV)

God accepted the sincere worship of those in attendance, and He blessed them. Among all the people of Israel who celebrated the feast, a great reformation took place. Those who took hold of the reformation went out to the cities to destroy the idols, images, groves and high places (2 Chron. 31:1).

Although this joyous event under the Davidic king Hezekiah must have been for many Israelites an impressive fulfillment of Hosea's words, we should consider that a later, even more impressive fulfillment took place under the pious Davidic king Josiah. This devoted king cleansed Israel and Judah of all idolatry and then brought the people together in joint celebration of the Passover. The chronicler of the event declared: "There had been no Passover kept in Israel like that since the days of Samuel the prophet; and none of the kings of Israel had kept such a Passover as Josiah kept, with the priests and the Levites, all Judah and Israel who were present, and the inhabitants of Jerusalem" (2 Chron. 35:18, NKJV).

Thus, the meaning and fulfillment of Hosea's message should not be projected into the far distant future in the last days with the assumption that Israel will then repent, be converted and restored. No, says the prophecy, after Israel has been many days without king, sacrifice and ephod, they will seek the Lord and David their king and will turn to God in the coming days. The *New English Bible* says: "… but after that they will again seek the LORD their God and David their king, and turn anxiously to the LORD for his bounty in days to come" (Hosea 3:5). As we have seen, this took place in the days of the Davidic kings Hezekiah and Josiah, and there is no reason to project a further turning to the Lord in the "last days," although some Bibles use these words. The same Hebrew words translated "last days" are also found in Genesis 49:1, where the context uses the phrase as meaning, in "the days to come," which would be in the lifespan of Jacob's sons. (See how "the last days" is also used to mean in "the days to come," in Deuteronomy 4:30 and Numbers 24:14.) In the same way, as we read Hosea 3:5, we need not think of the "last days" at the end of the world but in the days that followed the events and circumstances alluded to by the prophet when the prophecy was given.

The Old City of Jerusalem with Lutheran Church

The Ten Tribes and the Rebuilding of Israel

A large number of people hold to the belief that there remains a promise of return for the ten tribes. Since those who returned from the Babylonian captivity represent only a rather small remnant of the two tribes of Judah and Benjamin, the majority of Israel from the deported ten tribes are still waiting for their return. The thinking is that, since God's Word is infallible and God never promises anything that He would not do, the ten tribes must yet be gathered and experience a bright future of recovery.

Is it true that the promises of recovery for the ten tribes are yet without fulfillment?

The prophet Jeremiah, who can be called the prophet of the captivity, proclaimed that, after seventy years were accomplished at Babylon, the Lord would bring His people back to their country from all the nations and places to which they have been driven to enjoy a blessed and peaceful future (Jer. 29:10–14).

It was the Persian king Cyrus whose spirit was stirred up by God to send a proclamation throughout all his kingdom, as Ezra recorded: "In the first year of Cyrus king of Persia, that the word of the LORD BY THE MOUTH OF JEREMIAH MIGHT BE FULFILLED, THE LORD STIRRED UP THE SPIRIT OF CYRUS KING OF PERSIA, SO THAT HE MADE A PROCLAMATION THROUGHOUT ALL HIS KINGDOM AND ALSO PUT IT IN WRITING: 'Thus says Cyrus king of Persia: The LORD, the God of heaven, has given me all the kingdoms of the earth, and he has charged me to build him a house at Jerusalem, which is in Judah. Whoever is among you of all his people, may his God be with him, and let him go up to Jerusalem, which is in Judah, and rebuild the house of the LORD, the God of Israel—he is the God who is in Jerusalem'" (Ezra 1:1–3, ESV).

To whom was this proclamation addressed? Was it only to the two tribes of Judah and not to the ten tribes of Israel? We read in the proclamation: 'Whoever is among you of all his people …' This certainly includes all the people of Israel and Judah; all the twelve tribes. None of them is excluded. Without exception, they were all allowed to go up to Jerusalem.

Notice that Cyrus sent this proclamation throughout his whole kingdom—that is, all the countries and lands of the earth that the Lord God had given him. For this reason, it is hard to imagine a place where people would have been ignorant of his royal proclamation. The Persian kingdom was at that time—without a doubt—a great and mighty world empire, and the proclamation was made known in every part of it. Among those who returned to Jerusalem were also a number of people that "could not prove their fathers' houses or their descent, whether they belonged to Israel" (Ezra 2:59, ESV). If these people who had no genealogical record of their lineage could return to the Promised Land, then certainly all those who could show their lineage in the ten tribes of Israel would not have been excluded, but could, without a doubt, have returned as well. To restrict the call to return to only the two tribes of Judah and to project a return of the ten tribes in the far distant future during the time of the end is scripturally unwarranted.

The small number of dispersed Israelites who were willing to return was not limited to the ten tribes only. Many of the two tribes of Judah also preferred to stay in the places to which they had been scattered, in spite of the fact that God issued repeated calls to return. All Israel was called by God to return, but they were not forced to do so.

There was a willing remnant from the ten tribes who united with the willing remnant of the two tribes, and they worked together to rebuild the temple and the city of Jerusalem.

There was a willing remnant from the ten tribes who united with the willing remnant of the two tribes, and they worked together to rebuild the temple and the city of Jerusalem. The Persian kings Cyrus, Darius and Artaxerxes supported the returned exiles in their work. The king of Assyria also assisted them in the work on the house of God (Ezra 6:22).

Ezra informs us that, at the dedication of God's house, the priests offered "… as a sin offering for all Israel, twelve male goats, one for each of the tribes of Israel" (Ezra 6:17, NIV). This is further evidence that all twelve tribes were involved. Then, of the next group of exiles to arrive, we read: "Then the exiles who had returned from captivity sacrificed burnt offerings to the God of Israel: twelve bulls for all Israel … and, as a sin offering, twelve male goats" (Ezra 8:35, NIV). Thus, the return of the exiles was not restricted to a few tribes but involved representatives from all twelve tribes of Israel.

The completion of the temple and of the wall of Jerusalem, despite much opposition from the surrounding nations, was quite impressive. Nehemiah wrote: "When all our enemies heard about this, all the surrounding nations were afraid and lost their self-confidence, because they realized that this work had been done with the help of our God" (Neh. 6:16, NIV).

All the returned exiles celebrated the feasts, as prescribed in the book of the Law, and there was great rejoicing, as Nehemiah recorded: "And all the assembly of those who had returned from the captivity made booths and lived in the booths, for from the days of Jeshua the son of Nun to that day the people of Israel had not done so. And there was very great rejoicing" (Neh. 8:17, ESV). The prophets Haggai and Zechariah encouraged the people, assuring them that God was with them. They obeyed the voice of the Lord their God, and they all worked together as one (Hag. 1:12, 13). The promises that God then made to them were like those He made in days of old: "Therefore, thus says the LORD, 'I have returned to Jerusalem with mercy *and* compassion....' 'Proclaim again, "Thus says the LORD of hosts, 'My cities shall again overflow with prosperity, and the LORD shall again comfort Zion and again choose Jerusalem" ' " (Zech. 1:16, 17, AMP). Jerusalem will be a prosperous city with a multitude of people and cattle and the Lord God " 'will be a wall of fire around her [protecting her from enemies], and I will be the glory in her midst' " (Zech. 2:4, 5, AMP).

Notice also this encouraging description: "Thus saith the LORD of hosts; I was jealous for Zion with great jealousy, and I was jealous for her with great fury. Thus saith the LORD; I am returned unto Zion, and will dwell in the midst of Jerusalem: and Jerusalem shall be called a city of truth; and the mountain of the LORD of hosts the holy mountain. Thus saith the LORD of hosts; there shall yet old men and old women dwell in the streets of Jerusalem, and every man with his staff in his hand for very age. And the streets of the city shall be full of boys and girls playing in the streets thereof. Thus saith the LORD of hosts; If it be marvellous in the eyes of the remnant of this people in these days, should it also be marvellous in mine eyes? saith the LORD of hosts" (Zech. 8:2–6).

In light of these wonderful promises, is it still possible to assert that there will be another fulfillment in the last days? Notice that the Lord did return to Zion in those days. Notice also that the wonderful promises are said to be marvelous to the remnant in "these days" that is in *those days* when the prophet spoke God's comforting words after

Israel's remnant was returned from their captivity. Thus, there is no indication that there are another return and recovery of Israel to take place at the end of time to fulfill an evangelizing role during the millennial period.

Zechariah's Prophecy of the Future

Many people base their view of Israel's glorious recovery in the time of the end particularly upon the prophecies of Zechariah. Yet, the prophet did not refer to the distant future. Zechariah wrote:

> Thus saith the Lord of hosts; Let your hands be strong, ye that hear in these days these words by the mouth of the prophets, which *were* in the day *that* the foundation of the house of the Lord of hosts was laid, that the temple might be built.... But now I *will* not *be* unto the residue of this people as in the former days, saith the Lord of hosts. For the seed *shall be* prosperous; the vine shall give her fruit, and the ground shall give her increase, and the heavens shall give their dew; and I will cause the remnant of this people to possess all these *things*. And it shall come to pass, *that* as ye were a curse among the heathen, O house of Judah, and house of Israel; so will I save you, and ye shall be a blessing: fear not, *but* let your hands be strong. For thus saith the Lord of hosts; As I thought to punish you, when your fathers provoked me to wrath, saith the Lord of hosts, and I repented not: So again have I thought in these days to do well unto Jerusalem and to the house of Judah: fear ye not. (Zech. 8:9, 11–15)

God's promises of a blessed recovery for Israel were clearly meant for *"these days"*—that is, the days following the captivity, the very time in which the prophet was predicting Israel's recovery.

Is it possible, however, that Zechariah also spoke of a future scattering? It seems that one verse, as translated in some Bibles, supports this view: "And I will sow them among the people: and they shall remember me in far countries; and they shall live with their children, and turn again" (Zech. 10:9, KJV).

Other translations, such as the *Revised Standard Version*, the *English Standard Version* and the *Jerusalem Bible* use the perfect tense, which is a proper translation, according to the Hebrew. Consider just the reading of the *Jerusalem Bible:* "I have scattered them among the peoples ..." In the days of Zechariah, the first return of people under Zerubbabel had taken place. Yet, there were still many people who had not yet returned but would do so sometime in the future. Zechariah's messages were, therefore, meant to encourage people to return. Moreover, the following verse shows that the return spoken of was from the Assyrian-Babylonian captivity: "I will bring them home from the land of Egypt, and gather them from Assyria" (Zech. 10:10, ESV).

The surrounding nations offered great resistance against the work of rebuilding the city of Jerusalem and its temple. They did all they could to stop the work, but God was with His people. Zechariah's prediction was that God would "make Jerusalem a cup of trembling unto all the people round about, when they shall be in the siege both against Judah *and* against Jerusalem" (Zech. 12:2). This great encouragement soon became a reality in the days of Nehemiah. When the enemies heard that the repairs had gone ahead and the gaps of Jerusalem's walls were being closed up, they plotted in anger to fight against Jerusalem (Neh. 4:7, 8). Then, when Jerusalem's wall was completed, the surrounding nations were filled with fear and were greatly disheartened as they perceived that this marvelous work was accomplished by God's help (Neh. 6:16).

God did wonderful things for His people. Yet, sadly, during the coming years, they forgot the LORD their God and began again to walk in their own ways.

During the period of grace that God marked off for Israel, which lasted until the time of Jesus, God promised to be with them if they turned to Him. This was true when the pious Judas Maccabeus, in the face of great national apostasy, fought for God's sake and won, by God's help, one victory after another. The service of the temple, that had been interrupted by Antiochus Epiphanes, was restored and Israel's enemies were defeated. Under Simon Maccabeus, the Jews became a free and independent state in 142 BC.

If the Jewish people, after the captivity, would have maintained their faithfulness to God, they would have received manifold blessings and a glorious future.

If the Jewish people, after the captivity, would have maintained their faithfulness to God, they would have received manifold blessings and a glorious future. However, because of their renewed unfaithfulness, God could not protect His people or bless them as He would have liked.

God promised to pour out upon His people the spirit of grace and supplication. This would come about through the coming Messiah, who was full of "grace and truth" (John 1:17), and for whose appearance the faithful in Israel had long since been praying. Tragically, when He came to His people, it was not to their joy and happiness, for they turned their back to Him and even had Him pierced. Yet, one day they will mourn in bitterness for what they did to Him (Zech. 12:10; cf. Luke 6:25; Matt. 24:30). To the disobedient He will become a stone of stumbling and a rock of offense (1 Peter 2:8). Yet, not all of the Jews would reject Jesus as Messiah. There would be a faithful remnant. Zechariah prophesied that two parts of the land will be cut off and die, while one-third will be left and will be tried and refined. Zechariah declared: "They will call on My name, and I will answer them. I will say, 'This *is* My people'; and each one will say, 'The LORD *is* my God'" (Zech. 13:9, NKJV). These prophecies clearly indicate that not all of the people of Israel are God's people who will be saved. Only a faithful remnant (or "residue," KJV) of the people belongs to God and will be saved; only a remnant will not be cut off (Zech. 14:2).

It would be well for those who expect a glorious future on this earth for Israel to consider carefully that only a faithful remnant of Israel will claim God's promises. If Israel would have been faithful and accepted God's guidance to be a blessing among the nations, then God's promises would have become a reality in full measure and Israel's history *would have been* glorious. Jerusalem *would have been* a permanent city of worship for all nations.

However, because of Israel's renewed unfaithfulness, the promises of God will not find literal fulfillment in the earthly Jerusalem but in the heavenly New Jerusalem. As Paul explained, the earthly Jerusalem, with her children, has entered into a state of bondage, while the New Jerusalem above is free and mother of all those full of faith (Gal. 4:25, 26).

The final book of the Bible describes the New Jerusalem coming down from heaven and resting upon the earth as God's plan of salvation comes to an end. Then the resurrected, wicked nations will try to capture the city, but fire from heaven will destroy them all, and the Lord God will reign as King of the earth made new

(Zech. 14:8, 9, 12; Rev. 20:9; 21:1–3; 22:1–5). While all the disobedient will be destroyed, all the faithful redeemed will come to worship the King, the LORD of hosts, from Sabbath to Sabbath and new moon to new moon (Zech. 14:16; Isa. 66:23, 24).

What Makes the New Covenant New

The Lord God promised to make a new covenant with the house of Israel and with the house of Judah (Jer. 31:31–34). Because they despised God's covenant, violating its conditions and ten precepts, God sent His wayward children into captivity (2 Kings 17:15, 18–23; Ps. 78:10, 37, 61).

After the period of captivity, God returned with mercy and compassion to His people and renewed again His covenant with them. This new covenant, which took effect after Israel's captivity, was not limited to the period of recovery when God called them to return to the Promised Land to rebuild Jerusalem and the temple. God's promise of a new covenant extended to the time of the New Testament when Jesus came as the new covenant's mediator (Heb. 8:6–13).

A number of people want to apply the promise of a new covenant exclusively to the people of Israel and Judah and believe that the new covenant would become effective no earlier than the days of the end, when, as they believe, Israel returns to the land and is converted, accepting the Messiah as their Millennial King.

Is this interpretation correct? Is the prophesied new covenant promise not yet in effect? Will God make this new covenant with Israel during the time of the end, and will it be restricted to the Jewish nation?

It is well to pause for a moment and give some thought to God's covenant with fallen humanity. The covenant that God has always made with human beings has always been a covenant of grace, focusing on saving human beings and bringing them back into God's presence as newborn, sinless holy beings. Christ, as the promised Seed of the woman (Gen. 3:15), is the center of God's covenant of grace, and, to every obedient human being, He is the way, the truth and the life— *eternal* life (John 14:6). God's covenant of grace was established with Noah, a just and righteous man among his wicked generation (Gen. 6:9, 18). God promised that the earth would not be destroyed again by a flood, and He repeatedly places the bow in the cloud as a token of the covenant of His faithfulness (Gen. 9:11–17).

Again, because of the disobedience and unbelief of humanity, God established His covenant with faithful Abraham and gave circumcision as a token of the covenant of a willing heart (Deut. 10:16; Gen. 17:11). God promised Abraham's posterity that they would possess the land (Gen. 17:1–11). In Abraham's seed, which is Christ, all nations shall be blessed (Gen. 26:4; Gal 3:16).

At Sinai, God established His covenant with Israel as a nation. On condition of obedience, they would be God's chosen, holy nation (Exod. 19:5, 6). Yet, because of their unfaithfulness in the following years, breaking God's covenant, they were uprooted as captives from the Promised Land. When the time of their captivity came to a close, in answer to God's call, a faithful remnant returned, and God was with them and put the promise of the new covenant into effect for them. Was this covenant different from the one made with Israel's fathers at Sinai, or was it because Israel had broken the covenant that God promised a new covenant with the same terms?

We have noticed already that there is only one covenant of grace centered in Christ, the promised Seed, and, on behalf of fallen humanity, Christ, the promised Seed, would conquer the powers of darkness and sin and destroy the source of evil.

The faithful believers of old were looking forward to the promised Messiah, and they entered God's covenant by exercising faith in their coming Redeemer. The ratification of God's covenant with man was by the blood of Christ, when He offered Himself as a sacrifice for the sins of the world. The ratification of the covenant made with Israel at Sinai was with the blood of an animal sacrifice, but it prefigured the all-sufficient sacrifice of the Lamb of God. Thus, there is no real difference between it and the covenant made at Sinai (Heb. 9:18–20, NKJV).

The meaning of God's covenant, however, has broadened and deepened in the fulfilled work of Christ on earth and His mediatorial ministry in the heavenly sanctuary (Heb. 10:10; 8:1, 2).

With Christ's having entered the heavenly sanctuary as mediator of the new covenant, is it possible that the predicted new covenant is not yet in effect? No, that is impossible. If the new covenant were not yet in effect and without a covenant relationship with humanity, there would be no point to Christ's mediatorial work for humankind.

We should take note also that the Bible speaks of a *better* covenant already in effect: "But now He has obtained a more excellent ministry, inasmuch as He is also Mediator of a better covenant, which was established on better promises. For if that first *covenant* had been faultless, then no place would have been sought for a second" (Heb. 9:6, 7, NKJV).

God made no mistake in the provisions of the covenant He established with His people. No, the ten commandments of God's covenant (Exod. 34:28; Deut. 4:13) were faultless, but the *people's* promises could not be trusted. We read: "And all the people answered together, and said, All that the LORD hath spoken we will do" (Exod. 19:8). The people's promise lasted but a short time. Even as Moses left them to go up into the mount to receive the engraved tables of God's law, the people implored Aaron to make a golden calf, which they worshiped. The improvement of the second, or new, covenant is that people are expected to put their trust in *God's* promises instead of relying on their own ability to obey. God's promises are always sure, and the pledge of His new covenant is that He will provide those with a heart loyal to Him the power to obey Him, to conquer sin, and to become His children (2 Chron. 16:9, NKJV, ESV; John 1:12, KJV).

Jeremiah promised this new covenant while the period of captivity was still in progress. Yet, the covenant would be made with the house of Israel and the house of Judah in the days to come (Jer. 31:31) when they were called to return to the Promised Land. Then God would put His law in their heart and graciously and compassionately accept them again as their God. They, in turn, would be His people (vs. 33). He would also forgive their iniquity and remember their sin no more (vs. 34).

Because of their continued disobedience, Israel as a nation had broken God's covenant and were led into captivity that, through their bitter experience, they might turn back to God and learn to live up to His covenant.

Faithful individual believers among Israel—such as Daniel—could still remain in covenant relationship with God whom they trusted and served throughout the days of their affliction.

God makes this promised new covenant with every faithful believer, and Jesus is the covenant's mediator. He serves in the heavenly sanctuary in behalf of all penitent people who trust in Him. There is no reason nor indication to assert that this covenant will be put into effect for natural Israel as a nation in the time of the end.

Will Jerusalem Have a Glorious Recovery?

With the fixed order of nature as a point of comparison, the prophet Jeremiah explains that, accordingly, Israel will always remain a nation: " 'If this fixed order departs from before me, declares the LORD, then shall the offspring of Israel cease from being a nation before me forever.' Thus says the LORD: 'If the heavens above can be measured, and the foundations of the earth below can be explored, then I will cast off all the offspring of Israel for all that they have done, declares the LORD.' 'Behold, the days are coming, declares the LORD, when the city shall be rebuilt for the LORD ... It shall not be plucked up or overthrown anymore forever' " (Jer. 31:36–38, 40, ESV). Such were God's encouraging words to Israel while they were still in captivity. God's promises are just as sure as the laws of nature. God promised that, if the children of Israel would faithfully obey Him, He would provide them with a glorious future when they returned from captivity, and the rebuilt city of Jerusalem would remain forever. However, even if they do disobey Him and walk in their own ways, He will never reject and destroy those who faithfully serve Him along with the guilty. God will never cast off *all* the offspring of Israel, for there will be a faithful remnant that will share God's promises and be richly blessed. Unfortunately, Israel as a nation again became disobedient throughout the years. They rejected their Messiah when He came, and their city with the beautiful temple was destroyed by the Roman armies.

The Lord God, who knows "the end from the beginning" (Isa. 46:10), declared through the prophet Ezekiel that Jerusalem, in all her ways, was more corrupted than Sodom and Samaria (Ezek. 16:2, 46–52). Building on this comparison, Ezekiel explains that, if Sodom and Samaria would be restored to their former state, then Jerusalem would return to her former state. He declares: "When your sisters, Sodom and her daughters, return to their former state, and Samaria and her daughters return to their former state, then you and your daughters will return to your former state" (Ezek. 16:55, NKJV).

The *New English Bible* says: "... but when your sister Sodom and her daughters become what they were of old, and when your sister Samaria and her daughters become what they were of old, then you and your daughters will be restored" (Ezek. 16:55, NEB).

These words are without equivocation. A righteous and impartial God cannot and will not restore Jerusalem to its bright former state as it was in the days of David and Solomon, for Jerusalem's guilt is greater than that of Sodom and Samaria. God cannot justly benefit Jerusalem above these two cities with lesser guilt (cf. Matt. 10:15).

Was God possibly intimating that Sodom and Samaria will sometime be restored to their former flourishing state? If that is not imaginable, then neither is it imaginable that Jerusalem will again be

Part 3 Israel and the Old Testament 137

restored to a former state of prosperity, for God is righteous in all His ways, and there is not even a shadow of His favoring one above the other in His dealings with humankind.

Thus, let it be clear then, that if a righteous and impartial God would bring Jerusalem's children back again to their original glorious state, then He should, in all fairness, also bring back in their former state the children of Sodom and Samaria, who were less corrupt. Since Sodom and Samaria were less guilty, they would be raised up to their former state sooner than Jerusalem, which had more guilt, would be restored to her former glory.

If Sodom were to be raised up from the Dead Sea to her former glorious state, which is wholly inconceivable, then only would Jerusalem also be restored to her bright, ancient glory.

Some Bibles do not have the conditional aspect in verse 55, but simply say that Sodom and Samaria will return to their former state. This is, however, a problematic translation, for how is it even thinkable that this could ever be true? It certainly does not seem to be the sense of the passage, but it is the only way to support the notion that Jerusalem will one day be restored to her former glory.

While the Jews were still in Babylonian captivity, as a punishment for their sins, the prophet assured the people: " 'You have borne [the penalty of] your lewdness and your repulsive acts,' says the LORD. Yes, thus says the Lord GOD, 'I will also deal with you as you have done, you who have despised the oath by breaking the covenant' "

(Ezek. 16:58, 59, AMP). At the same time, God's messages of judgment were coupled with messages of hope. We read: "Nevertheless, I will restore them [again] from their captivity, the captivity of Sodom and her daughters (outlying cities), the captivity of Samaria and her daughters, and along with them [I will restore you from] your own captivity [in the day of the Lord GOD] ..." (Ezek. 16:53, AMP).

Babylon was a great and mighty world power in those days, and all the surrounding nations, cities and places—including Jerusalem, Samaria and the places in the region of Sodom—served the king of Babylon. Yet, when the predicted seventy years were complete, Babylon's yoke would be broken and the captivity would cease (Jer. 25:11; 27:6–8; 29:10).

From the foregoing, it is clear that God deals justly with all people. He does not favor Israel above other nations. After Israel has been duly punished, God will call them to return to the Promised Land, and, if they seek God with all their heart, He will be found (Jer. 29:12–14), and He will restore again His covenant with them. "Nevertheless, I will remember [with compassion] My covenant with you in the days of your youth, and I will establish an everlasting covenant with you" (Ezek. 16:60, AMP).

God's compassionate grace is absolute and wonderful. If His people had been faithful and obedient through the years, their history would have been—without any doubt—prosperous, bright and glorious.

God's compassionate grace is absolute and wonderful. If His people had been faithful and obedient through the years, their history would have been—without any doubt—prosperous, bright and glorious.

Yet, sadly, the nation of Israel rejected their Messiah. They filled up the measure of iniquity of their fathers, and the kingdom was taken away from them and given to another nation. Jesus declared that *their* house was left unto them desolate. Therefore, Israel will not be restored again to her former state as God's chosen nation—not any more than Sodom and Samaria will be restored. However, God will make His covenant with believing Jews, individually, and they will be a part of God's Israel of the Spirit, together with all other people who believe.

Dormition Abbey and Monastery of a Benedictine community in Jerusalem near the Zion Gate

God's Chosen People

The word of God is sure and will never fail. It will stand forever (Isa. 40:8). God's plan of redemption will succeed despite the disobedience of many people who do not walk in His ways. With God there is no variableness nor shadow of turning (James 1:17).

The faithful believers of old understood that the promises of God had a spiritual character. Although the land of promise was given them as a possession, they confessed that they were strangers and pilgrims on this earth. They looked for a heavenly country with a city prepared for them by God (Heb. 11:8–16). Paul wrote: "And all of these, though they gained [divine] approval through their faith, did not receive [the fulfillment of] what was promised, because God had us in mind *and* had something better for us, so that they [these men and women of authentic faith] would not be made perfect [that is, completed in Him] apart from us" (Heb. 11:39, 40, AMP).

This has always been God's plan. Salvation was never intended to be exclusively Israel's privilege. It was meant equally for all people. God is "not willing that any should perish, but that all should come to repentance" (2 Peter 3:9). All true believers from the Old Testament and from the New Testament are together be made perfect in Christ. They will "come from the east and west, and shall sit down with Abraham, and Isaac, and Jacob, in the kingdom of heaven" (Matt. 8:11). Through faith they are all brethren, and they are, like Isaac, the children of promise and heirs of the heavenly Jerusalem, which is free and mother of us all (Matt. 23:8; Gal. 4:26, 28).

Salvation was never intended to be exclusively Israel's privilege. It was meant equally for all people.

In harmony with the words of the prophets, God has chosen a people for His name from the Gentiles, who will rebuild the fallen tabernacle of David (Acts 15:14–16). They are no more strangers and foreigners but fellow-citizens of God's household. They have come in faith to Christ, the chief corner stone; as lively stones, they are built up a spiritual house, a holy temple in the Lord, upon the foundation laid by Christ (Eph. 2:19–22; 3:6; 1 Peter 2:4, 5). The prophet Zechariah refers to Christ as "THE BRANCH" who would build the temple of the Lord (Zech. 6:12), and he prophesied that they that are far off shall come and help build the temple of the Lord (vs. 15). This means that Gentile believers would be faithful co-workers with Christ as Isaiah prophesied: "And the sons of strangers shall build up thy walls ..." (Isa. 60:10). In this way, faithful Gentiles will rebuild the fallen house of David.

There is no afterthought with God. He has known what would happen from the very beginning, and His purpose has always been to save all who are willing to seek Him: "That the residue of men might seek after the Lord, and all the Gentiles, upon whom my name is called, saith the Lord, who doeth all these things. Known unto God are all his works from the beginning of the world" (Acts 15:17, 18).

With God's plan of salvation, all things known from the beginning fall into place: "And the scripture, foreseeing that God would justify the heathen through faith, preached before the gospel unto Abraham, *saying*, In thee shall all nations be blessed. So then they which be of faith are blessed with faithful Abraham" (Gal. 3:8, 9).

The apostle Peter wrote his first letter to the scattered *strangers*, or *aliens* (1 Peter 1:1, KJV, NASB). He identifies them as: "Elect according to the foreknowledge of God the Father, through sanctification of the Spirit, unto obedience and sprinkling of the blood of Jesus Christ ..." (vs. 2). Notice that Peter does not speak of *scattered Jews* as God's elect. No, as did Isaiah in a similar context (Isa. 60:10), he uses the word *strangers* who, as God's elect, have become faithful, sanctified and obedient co-workers with God. Peter emphasizes that all such believers "*are* a chosen generation, a royal priesthood, an holy nation, a peculiar people ... which in time past *were* not a people, but *are* now the people of God: which had not obtained mercy, but now have obtained mercy" (1 Peter 2:9, 10; cf. Exod. 19:5, 6). There is no question but that Peter is addressing *Gentiles* who had not been God's people but who had become so as faithful believers. He addresses them once again, in the following verse, as *strangers* and *pilgrims*: "Dearly beloved, I beseech *you* as strangers and pilgrims, abstain from fleshly lusts ..." (vs. 11).

Israel was God's firstborn son. The Gentile believers are God's other "son," who finally did the Father's will (Exod. 4:22; Matt. 21:28–32). Had not the prophet Amos already reprimanded Israel, indicating that the other nations were also God's children (Amos 9:7). The scalding message of the prophet Hosea declared that God would "never again show love to Israel; never again forgive them." They would not be God's people, and He would not be their God (Hosea 1:6, 9, NEB).

Because of their sins, God would reject Israel as a nation. Nonetheless, Hosea's message communicated hope as he spoke of Israel and Judah's restoration. Yet again, God's chosen nation did not live up to God's elevated plan for them and, although it would be fulfilled in a faithful remnant, it seems that the prophet hinted at a further fulfillment in those that were not God's people but of whom it shall be said, "You are sons of the living God" (Hosea 1:10, NKJV) The apostle Paul quoted Hosea's prophecy, applying it to God's other faithful children, for those called by God are "not of the Jews only but also of the Gentiles" (Rom. 9:24).

God has always been longsuffering towards His people. With a strong hand He led them out of Egypt into the Promised Land. On condition of obedience, He promised them many blessings. Once again, after the period of captivity, He raised His compassionate hand over His people, the house of Israel and the house of Judah, and gathered them, as one and the same commonwealth, from the four corners of the earth back into their land, and He promised them anew many blessings (Isa. 11:11–16; Jer. 3:18; 30:3; Ezek. 11:15–17; 37:11–14). Despite the spiritual adultery of His people, God promised that, after the captivity, He would betroth, in faithfulness and mercy, those who know Him (Hosea 2:19, 20). In actuality, after the captivity, Israel again committed spiritual adultery. As His last act of mercy, God sent His beloved Son, yet He was killed, and the vineyard was given to others (Mark 12:6–9).

The believers of the New Testament are now God's chosen nation, and God is jealous over them to betroth them to Christ as a chaste virgin (2 Cor. 11:2, NEB; cf. Hosea 2:19, 20).

The ingathering of all believers is only in and through Jesus Christ. God promised that others besides the Jews will be gathered in .

The ingathering of all believers is only in and through Jesus Christ. God promised that others besides the Jews will be gathered in (Isa. 56:8; John 10:16). His sad proclamation is that those who were bidden were not worthy. Therefore, the Master's servants are sent out into the highways to gather as many as will respond to their invitation (Matt. 22:8–10; 8:11, 12). Christ promised to draw all to Himself (John 12:32).

Jesus is preparing a place, and He will come again to gather the faithful unto Himself in His Father's house (John 14:2, 3). When He comes, His angels will be sent out "with a great sound of a trumpet, and they shall gather together his elect from the four winds, from one end of heaven to the other" (Matt. 24:31). Those who sleep in Christ will be raised to life, and, with the living saints, will be gathered unto Christ in the heavenly Canaan. Then, at the end of a thousand years, the city of God, the New Jerusalem, will come down from God out of heaven, and a new heaven and a new earth will remain into eternity the habitation of the redeemed, who are written in the Lamb's book of life (1 Thess. 4:13–17; Heb. 11:13–16, 39, 40; Rev. 3:12; 21:1–10, 22–27; 22:1–7; Isa. 65:17–19; 66:22, 23).

Amen. So be it. May your name be written in the book of the Lamb that you may sit down with Abraham, Isaac, and Jacob in the kingdom.

Appendix

The following are quotations that indicate that all twelve tribes returned as a blended unity after the Assyrian-Babylonian captivity.

> 1 Chron. IX:2. *The Israelites,* i.e. the common people of Judah and Israel, called here by the general name of *Israelites*, which was given to them before that unhappy division of the two kingdoms, and now is restored to them when the Israelites are united with the Jews in one and the same commonwealth, that so all the names and signs of their former division might be blotted out. And although the generality of the ten tribes were yet in captivity, yet divers of them were now returned; either such as had long before the captivity fled to Jerusalem to worship God, and joined themselves with Judah, as those 2 Chron. xi. 16, and others; or such as, upon Cyrus's general proclamation, associated themselves, and returned with those of Judah and Benjamin.[27]

> Ezra 2:70. **All Israel**. Ezra very determinately puts forward this aspect of the return—that it was participated in

---

[27] Matthew Poole, *A Commentary on the Holy Bible* (London: The Banner of Truth Trust, 1962), vol. 1, p. 789.

by all the tribes (see ii. 2; iii. 1; vi. 16, 17; vii. 13; viii. 29, 35, &c.).

Ezra 6:16. **The children of Israel.** Again the writer is careful to present the returned exiles to us as "Israel" and not merely "Judah" (comp. ii. 70; iii. 1, 10, 11; iv. 3; v. 1). This is especially fitting when he is about to explain why the number of the he-goats offered was twelve.[28]

Josephus says that the proclamation of Cyrus was sent to the descendants of the ten tribes living in Media under his dominion; and as it comprehended the whole nation, it is probable that the first caravan which went to Jerusalem comprised persons from all the tribes (see 1 Chron. ix. 3).[29]

Ezra 2:70. **All Israel in their cities.** Cf. Ezr. 2:2b. It is certain that all twelve tribes were represented in this expedition, for refugees from the northern tribes had been pouring into Judah for centuries before the Babylonian captivity.[30]

Ezra 2:64. **[T]he whole congregation together was forty-two thousand three hundred and threescore**—this gross amount is 12,000 more than the particular numbers given in the catalogue, when added together, come to. Reckoning up the smaller numbers, we shall find that they amount to 29,818 in this chapter, and to 31,089 in the parallel chapter of Nehemiah. Ezra also mentions 494 persons omitted by Nehemiah, and Nehemiah mentions 1765 not noticed by Ezra. If, therefore, Ezra's surplus be added to the sum in Nehemiah, and Nehemiah's surplus to the number in Ezra, they will both become 31,583. Subtracting this from 42,360, there will be a deficiency of 10,777. These are

---

28 H. D. M. Spence-Jones, Joseph S. Exell, Edward Mark Deems, ed., *The Pulpit Commentary* (Grand Rapids, MI: Wm. B. Eerdmans Publishing Co., 1950), vol. 7, pp. 24, 87.

29 C. H. Irwin, ed., *The Universal Bible Commentary* (London: The Religious Tract Society, 1928), p. 142.

30 Charles F. Pfeiffer, Everett F. Harrison, ed., *The Wycliffe Bible Commentary* (Chicago: Moody Press, 1962), p. 425.

omitted, because they did not belong to Judah and Benjamin, or to the priests, but to the other tribes.[31]

It is usually believed, that there was no general return of the ten tribes from this captivity; but the prophets seem to speak of the return of at least a great part of Israel. (See Hos. xi. 11; Amos ix. 14; Obad. 20; Isa xi. 12; Ezek. xxxvii. 16; Jer. xlvi. 27; xlix. 2, &c.; Micah ii. 12; Zech. ix. 13; x. 6, 10.) From the historical books we see that Israelites of the *ten tribes*, as well as of Judah and Benjamin, returned from the captivity. Among those who returned with Zerubbabel, are reckoned some of Ephraim and Manasseh, who settled at Jerusalem, among the tribe of Judah. When Ezra numbered those who had returned, he only required whether they were of the race of Israel; and at the first passover celebrated in the temple after the return, was a sacrifice of twelve he-goats for the whole house of Israel, according to the number of the tribes, Ezra vi. 16, 17; viii. 35. Under the Maccabees, and during the time of our Saviour, we see that Palestine was peopled by Israelites of all the tribes, indifferently. The Samaritan chronicle asserts, that in the 35th year of the pontificate of Abdelus, 3000 Israelites, by permission of king Sauredius, returned from captivity, under the conduct of Adus, son of Simeon.[32]

In the New Testament we read of the entire body of the twelve tribes as still subsisting and waiting on the service of God, Ac. xxvi. 7; Ja. i. 1.[33]

Ezra 2:70. *All Israel.*] That Israelites of the Ten Tribes returned to Palestine with Zerubbabel is apparent, 1. from the statement in 1 Chr. ix. 3; 2. from the enumeration of

---

31   Robert Jamieson, Andrew Robert Fausset, David Brown, *Commentary Practical and Explanatory on the Whole Bible* (Hartford, CT: S. S. Scranton & Co., 1871), vol. 1, 289.

32   Edward Robinson, *The Comprehensive Critical and Explanatory Bible Encyclopaedia* (Toledo, OH: O. A. Browning & Co., 1881), p. 275.

33   Patrick Fairbairn, ed., *Imperial Standard Bible Encyclopedia* (Grand Rapids, MI: Zondervan Publishing House, 1957), vol. 1, p. 349.

twelve chiefs (Neh. vii. 7; 1 Esd. v. 8); and 3. from various expressions in Ezra (see ii. 2, 59, iii. 1; &c.).[34]

But it is a harsh assumption that such intermarriage were commoner with the ten tribes than with the two; and certainly, in the apostolic days, the *twelve* tribes are referred to as a well-known people, sharply defined from the heathen (Acts xxiv: 7; James i: 1). Not a trace appears that any repulsive principle existed at that time between the Ten and the Two. "Ephraim no longer envied Judah, nor Judah vexed Ephraim;" but they had become "one nation;" though only partially "on the mountains of Israel" (Is. xi, 13; Ezek. xxxvii, 22). It would seem, therefore, that the result of the captivity was to blend all the tribes together, and produce a national union which had never been effected in their own land. If ever there was a difference between them as to the books counted sacred, that difference entirely vanished; at least, no evidence appears of the contrary fact. When, moreover, the laws of landed inheritance no longer enforced the maintenance of separate tribes and put a difficulty in the way of their intermarriage, an almost inevitable result in course of time was the entire obliteration of this distinction; and, as a fact, no modern Jews know to what tribe they belong, although vanity always makes them choose to say that they are of the two or three, and not of the ten tribes.[35]

1. The Israelites. That general name is used (*v*. 2) because with those of Judah and Benjamin there were many of Ephraim and Manasseh, and the other ten tribes (*v*. 3), such as had escaped to Judah when the body of the ten tribes were carried captive or returned to Judah upon the revolutions in Assyria, and so went into captivity with them, or met them when they were in Babylon, associated with them, and so shared in the benefit of their enlargement. It was foretold that the *children of Judah and of Israel* should be *gathered together and come up out of the*

---

34   F. C. Cook, *The Holy Bible According to the Authorized Version (AD 1611) with an Explanatory and Critical Commentary and a Revision of the Translation* (New York: Charles Scribner's Sons, 1891), vol. 3, pp. 395, 396.

35   John McClintock, James Strong, *Cyclopædia of Biblical, Theological, and Ecclesiastical Literature* (New York: Harper & Brothers Publishers, 1891), vol. 8, p. 1052

land (Hos. i. 11), and that they should be one nation again, Ezek. xxxvii. 22. Trouble drives them together that have been at variance; and the pieces of metal that had been separated will run together again when melted in the same crucible. Many both of Judah and Israel staid [*sic*] behind in captivity; but some of both, whose spirits God stirred up, enquired the way to Zion again. Divers are here named, and many more numbered, who were *chief of the fathers* (*v.* 9), who ought to be remembered with honour, as Israelites indeed.[36]

[1 Chron. 9:]2. *Now the first inhabitants that dwelt*] Here follows an account of those who returned into their own land with Zerubbabel upon the decree of Cyrus, 2 Chron. xxxvi. 22, 23. They were divided, as is here expressed, into four descriptions of persons. The first are Israelites, that is, some of the ten tribes who were carried into Assyria and Media, and now chose to come back with their brethren of Judah.

[1 Chron. 9:]3. – *children of Ephraim, and Manasseh:*] We have here a plain proof that many out of those tribes returned from Babylon, together with the tribe of Judah. *Dr. Wall.*

[Ezra 6:]17. – *twelve he goats, according to the number of the tribes*] We are here supplied with an additional proof that, on the return of the tribes of Judah and Benjamin from the Babylonish captivity, many also of each of the other tribes returned with them from Assyria, Babylonia, and Media, whither they had been carried; and, joining with them in the rebuilding of the temple, partook in the solemnity of the dedication; otherwise, there is no reason why the sin offering should now be offered in behalf of all the twelve tribes. Since, however, the greater part of those who returned, consisted of the tribe of Judah, their name swallowed up the names of all the rest; for, from this time, the whole people of Israel, of what tribe soever they were,

---

36   Matthew Henry, *An Exposition of the Old and New Testament: Wherein Each Chapter is Summed* (London: Joseph Robinson, 1839), vol. 2, p. 860.

began to be called Jews, and by that name they have been known ever since all the world over. *Dean Prideaux.*[37]

Israel, Kingdom of. ... Thus after a duration of two hundred and fifty-three years the kingdom of the ten tribes came to an end. They were scattered throughout the East.... Judah held its ground against Assyria for yet one hundred and twenty-three years, and became the rallying-point of the dispersed of every tribe, and eventually gave its name to the whole race. Those of the people who in the last struggle escaped into the territories of Judah or other neighbouring countries naturally looked to Judah as the head and home of their race. And when Judah itself was carried off to Babylon, many of the exiled Israelites joined them from Assyria, and swelled that immense population which made Babylonia a second Palestine.

Exile.... When Cyrus granted permission to the Jews to return to their own land (Ezra 1:5; 7:13), only a comparatively small number at first availed themselves of the privilege. It cannot be questioned that many belonging to the kingdom of Israel ultimately joined the Jews under Ezra, Zerubbabel, and Nehemiah, and returned along with them to Jerusalem (Jer. 50:4, 5, 17–20, 33–35).

Captivity.... In the first year of his reign as king of Babylon (B.C. 536), Cyrus issued a decree liberating the Jewish captives, and permitting them to return to Jerusalem and rebuild the city and the temple (2 Chr. 36:22, 23; Ezra 1; 2). The number of the people forming the first caravan, under Zerubbabel, amounted in all to 42,360 (Ezra 2:64, 65), besides 7,367 men-servants and maid-servants. A considerable number, 12,000 probably, from the ten tribes who had been carried away into Assyria no doubt combined with this band of liberated captives.[38]

"The Return and Reorganization Under Zerubbabel. Ezra 1-6" The genealogy in the second chapter gives only the heads of the vari-

---

37   George D'Oyly, Richard Mant, *The Holy Bible: With Notes, Explanatory and Practical* (Oxford: Clarendon Press, 1818), vol. 1, pp. vi, vii, xcv.

38   Matthew George Easton, ed., *Illustrated Bible Dictionary and Treasury of Biblical History, Biography, Geography, Doctrine and Literature* (London: T. Nelson & Sons, 1894), pp. 350, 351, 243, 126.

ous tribes or representatives of them: this list had been carefully preserved through the Exile. This company of returning pilgrims is the "remnant" so frequently spoken of by the prophet Isaiah. The total number was 42,360 Jews, and 7,337 servants. Their beasts numbered 736 horses, 250 mules, 435 cattle, 6,720 asses—a large caravan. The mention of the actual heads of the tribes in Ezra 2:2 and Nehemiah 7:7, gives evidence that the twelve tribes were represented in this return, the prophetic proof of which is found in Jeremiah 3:18; 16:15; 30:3; Ezekiel 11:15, 17. These prophecies show that Israel and Judah both were to return to their land. There is also abundant historical proof that Israel returned with Judah. After the division of the kingdom and before the captivity of Israel there were four defections from Israel to Judah. Then the history of the Jews after their return proves it (see Zech. 11:14); the twelve tribes were there in Christ's day, and James addresses the twelve tribes.[39]

---

39 J. B. Cranfill, ed., B. H. Carrol, *An Interpretation of the English Bible, The Divided Kingdom and Restoration Period* (Nashville, TN: Broadman Press, 1948), vol. 6, pp. 217, 218.

We invite you to view the complete
selection of titles we publish at:

www.TEACHServices.com

scan with your mobile
device to go directly
to our website

Please write or email us your praises, reactions, or
thoughts about this or any other book we publish at:

Info@TEACHServices.com

TEACH Services, Inc., titles may be purchased in bulk for
educational, business, fund-raising, or sales promotional use.
For information, please e-mail:

BulkSales@TEACHServices.com

Finally if you are interested in seeing
your own book in print, please contact us at

publishing@TEACHServices.com

We would be happy to review your manuscript for free.

www.ingramcontent.com/pod-product-compliance
Lightning Source LLC
Chambersburg PA
CBHW071212160426
43196CB00011B/2273